KEATS' WELL-READ URN:

An Introduction to Literary Method

Harvey T. Lyon
University of Pennsylvania

> *If we wish to know the force of human genius we should read Shakespeare. If we wish to see the insignificance of human learning we may study his commentators.*
> William Hazlitt

> *Before it is anything else, a poem is an expression in the form of words, and words do not contain their own meaning.*
> Earl Wasserman

> *The judgment that a passage is good is an act of living.*
> I. A. Richards

HENRY HOLT AND COMPANY   NEW YORK

25400-0118
Printed in the United States of America

For you, Yolanda

Copyright Acknowledgments

Oxford University Press for permission to reprint selections from *Letters of John Keats* edited by Frederick Page, World Classics Edition; from *The Poetical Works of John Keats* (1939 and 1956 editions) and *Keats* by H. W. Garrod; and from *Oxford Lectures on Poetry* by Ernest de Sélincourt.

Phoenix House Limited for permission to reprint a selection from *John Keats: an Introduction and a Selection* by Richard Church.

PMLA for selections from "Poetry of Sensation or of Thought?" by John Hawley Roberts, *PMLA*, XLV (1930); and "Keats's Ideal in the *Ode On A Grecian Urn*," by Jacob D. Wigod, *PMLA*, LXXII (March, 1957).

Prentice-Hall, Inc. for a selection from *A Grammar of Motives* by Kenneth Burke, pp. 461-462. Copyright 1945 by Prentice-Hall, Inc., Englewood Cliffs, N.J. Reprinted by permission of the publisher.

Routledge & Kegan Paul Ltd. for permission to reprint a selection from *Mencius on the Mind* by I. A. Richards.

Alfred Saifer for permission to reprint a selection from *The Romantic Quest* by H. N. Fairchild.

Charles Scribner's Sons for permission to reprint selections from *The Poetical Works and Other Writings of John Keats,* edited by H. Buxton Forman and Maurice Forman.

The Sewanee Review for permission to reprint a selection from "Trompe-L'Oeil in Shakespeare and Keats," by Robert M. Adams, LXI (1953).

Stanford University Press for permission to reprint a selection from *The Prefigurative Imagination of John Keats* by Newell Ford.

Alan Swallow, Publisher, for permission to reprint a selection from *On the Limits of Poetry: Selected Essays* by Allen Tate. Copyright 1948 by Allen Tate.

The University of California Press for permission to reprint a selection from *Major Adjectives in English Poetry from Wyatt to Auden* by Josephine Miles.

The University of Michigan Press for permission to reprint a selection from *Essays and Studies in English and Comparative Literature* by S. F. Gingerich.

The University of North Carolina Press for permission to reprint a selection from *The Imagery of Keats and Shelley: A Comparative Study* by Richard Harter Fogle.

University of Toronto Quarterly for selections from "The Character and Poetry of Keats" by Archibald Lampman, edited by E. K. Brown, reprinted by permission of Margaret Brown and Mrs. T. R. Loftus MacInnis; and from "Aesthetic Pattern in Keats' Odes" by Herbert Marshall McLuhan, reprinted by permission of H. M. McLuhan.

Wolfson, Lester Marvin for a selection from "A Rereading of Keats's Odes: The Intrinsic Approach in Literary Criticism" by Lester Marvin Wolfson.

Preface

In this book, an attempt has been made to introduce the student to poetry through criticism and to criticism through poetry; and further, to introduce the student to the techniques and results of serious (and occasionally frivolous) scholarship. The most abstruse scholarly works are here applied to the teaching of poetry in the freshman or sophomore classroom, a goal usually more wished for than expected.

The Keats ode was chosen, quite simply, because it is well-known, because it has tantalized generations of readers, and because (it sometimes seemed) nearly everyone who published a book after 1820 undertook to establish a final reading. That no final reading is either possible or desirable is, I feel, the ultimate insight available to the joyously serious reader of poetry. But the evidence here assembled—textual, scholarly, critical, covering 135 years—does not invite the complacency of either-or, the conclusion that the understanding of poetry is "merely" a matter of opinion, that what cannot be shown to be *a* must necessarily be whatever combination of letter-abstractions an individual reader assigns to it. Aldous Huxley quotes the saying of a Zen master: "Do not seek after truth, only cease to cherish opinion." If the student is able to accomplish this, he will perhaps have stumbled onto that kind of maturity which is the mark, I think, of the ode from beginning to enigmatic end.

The text may also be described as an example of the Controlled Material Research Method. Both primary and secondary sources are offered in abundance; no apparatus has been attached; the teacher, thus, may use as much or as little as he wishes without the frustrating sense that he must submit to another's method or fight it at every step.

My debts to teachers, scholars, friends are many. I cannot name them here; nor am I able to cite individually the members of several classes at the University of Kansas who made some of the most searching and fruitful comments and suggestions.

H.T.L.

November, 1957
University of Pennsylvania.

Contents

CHAPTER ONE

THE POEM

Introduction

The king, so the story goes, charmed by a poet's work, turned and ordered his treasurer to make a large gift to the poet; the treasurer, in a loud stage whisper, asked, "All this for a song?" The incredulous treasurer and many present-day college students share at least one attitude, then. Both feel poetry is all very well in its place, but that its place is somewhere that demands either less money or less time— in both cases, less of oneself. Without making any attempt to flatter its holders, one may call this an old, distinct, and popular theory of poetic value. One purpose of this book is to test in practice how good that theory is.

Most people today are simply not used to thinking of poetry as a serious activity worthy of time and effort. What they know of poetry, for the most part, is what they hear in the way of tricky verse trying to persuade them that of two soaps in all respects alike (including manufacturer) except for brand name, they should in- variably choose one. Or they know hymns but also have a vague sense that groups of words ending in rhymes are sometimes used for purposes not completely suitable to a church. Or, most probably, they know the lyrics of a steady succession of popular songs. What they do not know is the truth of what Emerson said:

> See the power of national emblems. Some stars, lilies, leopards, a crescent, a lion, an eagle, or other figure which came into credit God knows how, on an old rag of bunting, blowing in the wind on a fort at the end of the earth, shall make the blood tingle under the rudest or the most conventional exterior. The people fancy they hate poetry, and they are all poets and mystics!

1

When Thoreau, describing the benefits of walking, spoke of it as being "so sanative, so poetic," he coupled together two words we do not ordinarily think of as bearing any very intimate relation to one another. But Thoreau was a man who knew what he was talking about. In our time, the importance of poetry, very simply, is that it offers the opportunity for a healthy totality of response very few things around us permit. For poetry, I. A. Richards observed, "is the completest mode of utterance." That form of speech which uses every resource of language must inevitably say more than any other form; and the reader who is able to hear more or less fully what is being said is using, in the same degree, every resource he possesses.

But what is it he is hearing? What should he listen for? How shall he use what he hears? One way to begin an answer to these questions is to offer a poem to be listened to, and then to offer a series of examples of what various listeners, expert and amateur, have heard. When a man says, "I don't pretend to know anything about art, but I know what I like," he is enunciating another old, distinct, and popular theory of artistic value. But the remark is defensive; for what he is saying is that if he did know anything about art, his judgments might well be different, and that though he has a sense that ignorance is not the basis of wisdom, he will stick by his ignorance and take on all comers. But he is also saying something much more serious: that only when anything is cut down to his own size can he deal with it. Those of you who have had to deal with a parent or a supply sergeant who fitted you to clothes on such a principle will know how uncomfortable, not to say maddening, such a system can be physically. The discomfort to the spirit is a little less obvious and a lot more serious: your body, in the wrong-sized clothes, doesn't shrink; your mind does.

In this book, you will find a group of odes by John Keats. The first of them, "Ode on a Grecian Urn," is one of the most famous poems of the last century, and, indeed, of any century. To help you to hear what it says, critical and scholarly material of the most diverse sorts has been chosen: you will find it being discussed in relation to the general subject of poetry and Greek art, or classical literature, to psychological theories of Keats' day and ours, to the numbers and proportions of his use of adjectives, to mysticism; at least one of the critics is self-confident enough to do more than merely point out the bad lines in the poem, and goes on to offer you his own improvements; the critics and scholars are from all parts of the world; their work covers a period of almost a century and a half. Some of what they write is inevitably the result of folly, as some of it is happily the creation of wisdom. The disputes and disagreements have ranged over nearly every field of learning; to begin at the beginning, not only the actual wording but even the punctuation of the poem has not been satisfactorily determined. As you will see, the punctuation of the last lines of the poem is a peculiarly baffling and fascinating subject.

In order to present as much evidence as possible, I have edited the poem fully; that is, I have shown all the variant readings among the versions printed during Keats' life and among the longhand copies made by his friends. There is no copy of the poem in Keats' own hand. The remaining poems appeared in the same volume as did the "Ode on a Grecian Urn," that of 1820, except for the last, "Ode on Indolence." The latter was composed during the same period as the others, but Keats, for reasons we do not know, chose not to publish it.

The definitive edition of Keats is that of H. W. Garrod, published with a full textual apparatus in 1939, and reissued in a revised version, without most of the apparatus, by the Oxford University Press in 1956. Authority for all variant readings is based on the earlier text; the text of the poem itself is based on the 1956 edition, in which Mr. Garrod saw fit to make a very important change, discussed in the note to lines 49 and 50 of the poem.

There are three different kinds of sources for the text of the poem: 1) It appeared, anonymously, in *Annals of the Fine Arts*, No. XV, for January, 1820 (?). 2) It exists in the following transcripts: British Museum Ms. Egerton 2780, hereafter referred to as *E*, a notebook which was the property of George Keats; added to Charles Armitage Brown's *Life of John Keats* (hereafter referred to as *T*), in Brown's hand, are the first four stanzas of the poem; an additional collection, discovered after *T* had been bound, and hereafter referred to as *T²*, contains the fifth stanza; the Woodhouse Transcripts, hereafter referred to as *W²*; the transcripts in the Dilke copy of *Endymion*, hereafter referred to as *End*. 3) It appeared in the 1820 volume, *Lamia, Isabella, The Eve of St. Agnes, and Other Poems*, the third and last volume of his poems published during Keats' lifetime.

The Texts

Ode on a Grecian Urn

I

THOU still unravish'd bride of quietness,
　Thou foster-child of silence and slow time,
Sylvan historian, who canst thus express
　A flowery tale more sweetly than our rhyme:
What leaf-fring'd legend haunts about thy shape　5
　Of deities or mortals, or of both,
　　In Tempe or the dales of Arcady?
　What men or gods are these? What maidens loth?
What mad pursuit? What struggle to escape?
　　What pipes and timbrels? What wild ecstasy?　10

II

Heard melodies are sweet, but those unheard
　Are sweeter; therefore, ye soft pipes, play on;
Not to the sensual ear, but, more endear'd,
　Pipe to the spirit ditties of no tone:
Fair youth, beneath the trees, thou canst not leave　15
　Thy song, nor ever can those trees be bare;
　　Bold Lover, never, never canst thou kiss,
Though winning near the goal—yet, do not grieve;
　She cannot fade, though thou hast not thy bliss,
　　For ever wilt thou love, and she be fair!　20

III

Ah, happy, happy boughs! that cannot shed
　Your leaves, nor ever bid the Spring adieu;
And, happy melodist, unwearied,
　For ever piping songs for ever new;
More happy love! more happy, happy love!　25
　For ever warm and still to be enjoy'd,
　　For ever panting, and for ever young;
All breathing human passion far above,
　That leaves a heart high-sorrowful and cloy'd,
　　A burning forehead, and a parching tongue.　30

IV

Who are these coming to the sacrifice?
  To what green altar, O mysterious priest,
Lead'st thou that heifer lowing at the skies,
  And all her silken flanks with garlands drest?
What little town by river or sea shore,   35
    Or mountain-built with peaceful citadel,
      Is emptied of this folk, this pious morn?
And, little town, thy streets for evermore
    Will silent be; and not a soul to tell
      Why thou art desolate, can e'er return.   40

V

O Attic shape! Fair attitude! with brede
  Of marble men and maidens overwrought,
With forest branches and the trodden weed;
  Thou, silent form, dost tease us out of thought
As doth eternity: Cold Pastoral!   45
    When old age shall this generation waste,
      Thou shalt remain, in midst of other woe
Than ours, a friend to man, to whom thou say'st,
    'Beauty is truth, truth beauty,'—that is all
      Ye know on earth, and all ye need to know.   50

Textual notes for "Ode on a Grecian Urn."

Title: Ode on a Grecian Urn *1820 E T W²* End: On a Grecian Urn
    Annals.
Line   1   still, *Annals.*
       8   Gods or Men *Annals.*
       9   What mad pursuit? *1820:* What love? what dance *all*
MSS. and Annals.
     10   Extacy *End.*
     14   Spirit—ditties *T.*
     16   can those trees be bare] bid the spring adieu *Annals.*
     18   yet *1820:* O *all Mss. and Annals.*
     19   tho' *T End.*

22   never *Annals.*

28   All breathing, human *W².*

33   at *made out of* to W².

34   flanks *1820:* sides *all MSS. and Annals.*

37   *this 1820 E T W² End. Annals:* this *made out of* its (?) [W¹ for W², Garrod, 1939]: its *ed. Smith 1840.*

40   ne'er *End.*

42   maidens overwrought, *1820 Annals:* maidens, overwrought *E T² W² End.*

47   *shalt 1820:* wilt *E T² W² End. Annals.*

48   a *1820 End. Annals:* as *E W² T².*

49-50   These last two lines have occasioned more debate than almost any other lines of poetry in English, and the question of their punctuation is part of the dispute. It is the general practice of editors to take as a final text the last appearance of a poem during the poet's lifetime, unless there is a demonstrably later autograph revision. In the case of this poem, there is no autograph version of any kind. The last great editor before Dr. Garrod, Mr. H. Buxton Forman, therefore, accepted the 1820 volume reading of these two lines:

> "Beauty is Truth, Truth Beauty,"—that is all
> Ye know on earth, and all ye need to know.

None of the manuscript versions shows any quotation mark, nor does the version published in *Annals*. The latter, thus, reads:

> Beauty is Truth, Truth Beauty.—That is all
> Ye know on Earth, and all ye need to know.

In his earlier edition, Dr. Garrod chose to follow the authority of the manuscripts, supported in the main by the *Annals* printing, and rejected what would normally be accepted as the definitive reading, that of the 1820 volume. In his 1956 revised version, he adopted the 1820 reading which is given here. On neither occasion did he undertake to explain his decision. The difference between the two readings is obvious, and forms a part of many of the discussions in Chapter Three. You will notice that most of the older critics were not very precise in textual matters, and that many modern critics choose to follow the *Annals* version. For discussions of this question, see especially the selections by Forman, Wasserman, Tillotson, and Whitley in Chapter Three.

Ode to a Nightingale

I

My heart aches, and a drowsy numbness pains
  My sense, as though of hemlock I had drunk,
Or emptied some dull opiate to the drains
  One minute past, and Lethe-wards had sunk:
'Tis not through envy of thy happy lot,   5
  But being too happy in thine happiness,—
    That thou, light-winged Dryad of the trees,
      In some melodious plot
  Of beechen green, and shadows numberless,
    Singest of summer in full-throated ease.   10

II

O, for a draught of vintage! that hath been
  Cool'd a long age in the deep-delved earth,
Tasting of Flora and the country green,
  Dance, and Provençal song, and sunburnt mirth!
O for a beaker full of the warm South,   15
  Full of the true, the blushful Hippocrene,
    With beaded bubbles winking at the brim,
      And purple-stained mouth;
  That I might drink, and leave the world unseen,
    And with thee fade away into the forest dim: 20

III

Fade far away, dissolve, and quite forget
  What thou among the leaves hast never known,
The weariness, the fever, and the fret
  Here, where men sit and hear each other groan;
Where palsy shakes a few, sad, last gray hairs,   25
  Where youth grows pale, and spectre-thin, and dies;
    Where but to think is to be full of sorrow
      And leaden-eyed despairs,
  Where Beauty cannot keep her lustrous eyes,
    Or new Love pine at them beyond to-morrow.   30

IV

Away! away! for I will fly to thee,
  Not charioted by Bacchus and his pards,
But on the viewless wings of Poesy,
  Though the dull brain perplexes and retards:
Already with thee! tender is the night,   35
  And haply the Queen-Moon is on her throne,
    Cluster'd around by all her starry Fays;
      But here there is no light,
  Save what from heaven is with the breezes blown
    Through verdurous glooms and winding mossy ways.   40

V

I cannot see what flowers are at my feet,
  Nor what soft incense hangs upon the boughs,
But, in embalmed darkness, guess each sweet
  Wherewith the seasonable month endows
The grass, the thicket, and the fruit-tree wild;   45
  White hawthorn, and the pastoral eglantine;
    Fast fading violets cover'd up in leaves;
      And mid-May's eldest child,
  The coming musk-rose, full of dewy wine,
    The murmurous haunt of flies on summer eves.   50

VI

Darkling I listen; and, for many a time
  I have been half in love with easeful Death,
Call'd him soft names in many a mused rhyme,
  To take into the air my quiet breath;
Now more than ever seems it rich to die,   55
  To cease upon the midnight with no pain,
    While thou art pouring forth thy soul abroad
      In such an ecstasy!
  Still wouldst thou sing, and I have ears in vain—
    To thy high requiem become a sod.   60

VII

Thou wast not born for death, immortal Bird!
  No hungry generations tread thee down;

The voice I hear this passing night was heard
  In ancient days by emperor and clown:
Perhaps the self-same song that found a path   65
    Through the sad heart of Ruth, when, sick for home.
      She stood in tears amid the alien corn;
        The same that oft-times hath
    Charm'd magic casements, opening on the foam
    Of perilous seas, in faery lands forlorn.   70

VIII

Forlorn! the very word is like a bell
  To toll me back from thee to my sole self!
Adieu! the fancy cannot cheat so well
  As she is fam'd to do, deceiving elf.
Adieu! adieu! thy plaintive anthem fades   75
    Past the near meadows, over the still stream,
      Up the hill-side; and now 'tis buried deep
        In the next valley-glades:
    Was it a vision, or a waking dream?
      Fled is that music:—Do I wake or sleep?   80

Ode to Psyche

O GODDESS! hear these tuneless numbers, wrung
  By sweet enforcement and remembrance dear,
And pardon that thy secrets should be sung
  Even into thine own soft-conched ear:
Surely I dreamt to-day, or did I see   5
  The winged Psyche with awaken'd eyes?
I wander'd in a forest thoughtlessly,
  And, on the sudden, fainting with surprise,
Saw two fair creatures, couched side by side
    In deepest grass, beneath the whisp'ring roof   10
    Of leaves and trembled blossoms, where there ran
      A brooklet, scarce espied:

'Mid hush'd, cool-rooted flowers, fragrant-eyed,
  Blue, silver-white, and budded Tyrian,
They lay calm-breathing on the bedded grass;   15

Their arms embraced, and their pinions too;
Their lips touch'd not, but had not bade adieu,
As if disjoined by soft-handed slumber,
And ready still past kisses to outnumber
    At tender eye-dawn of aurorean love: 20
       The winged boy I knew;
    But who wast thou, O happy, happy dove?
       His Psyche true!

O latest born and loveliest vision far
    Of all Olympus' faded hierarchy!   25
Fairer than Phœbe's sapphire-region'd star,
    Or Vesper, amorous glow-worm of the sky;
Fairer than these, though temple thou hast none,
    Nor altar heap'd with flowers;
Nor virgin-choir to make delicious moan   30
    Upon the midnight hours;
No voice, no lute, no pipe, no incense sweet
    From chain-swung censer teeming;
No shrine, no grove, no oracle, no heat
    Of pale-mouth'd prophet dreaming.   35

O brightest! though too late for antique vows,
    Too, too late for the fond believing lyre,
When holy were the haunted forest boughs,
    Holy the air, the water, and the fire;
Yet even in these days so far retir'd   40
    From happy pieties, thy lucent fans,
    Fluttering among the faint Olympians,
I see, and sing, by my own eyes inspir'd.
So let me be thy choir, and make a moan
    Upon the midnight hours;   45
Thy voice, thy lute, thy pipe, thy incense sweet
    From swinged censer teeming;
Thy shrine, thy grove, thy oracle, thy heat
    Of pale-mouth'd prophet dreaming.

Yes, I will be thy priest, and build a fane   50
    In some untrodden region of my mind,
Where branched thoughts, new grown with pleasant pain,

Instead of pines shall murmur in the wind:
Far, far around shall those dark-cluster'd trees
 Fledge the wild-ridged mountains steep by steep; 55
And there by zephyrs, streams, and birds, and bees,
 The moss-lain Dryads shall be lull'd to sleep;
And in the midst of this wide quietness
A rosy sanctuary will I dress
With the wreath'd trellis of a working brain, 60
 With buds, and bells, and stars without a name,
With all the gardener Fancy e'er could feign,
 Who breeding flowers, will never breed the same:
And there shall be for thee all soft delight
 That shadowy thought can win, 65
A bright torch, and a casement ope at night,
 To let the warm Love in!

To Autumn

I

SEASON of mists and mellow fruitfulness,
 Close bosom-friend of the maturing sun;
Conspiring with him how to load and bless
 With fruit the vines that round the thatch-eves run;
To bend with apples the moss'd cottage-trees, 5
 And fill all fruit with ripeness to the core;
  To swell the gourd, and plump the hazel shells
 With a sweet kernel; to set budding more,
And still more, later flowers for the bees,
Until they think warm days will never cease, 10
  For Summer has o'er-brimm'd their clammy cells.

II

Who hath not seen thee oft amid thy store?
 Sometimes whoever seeks abroad may find
Thee sitting careless on a granary floor,
 Thy hair soft-lifted by the winnowing wind; 15
Or on a half-reap'd furrow sound asleep,
 Drows'd with the fume of poppies, while thy hook
  Spares the next swath and all its twined flowers:

And sometimes like a gleaner thou dost keep
  Steady thy laden head across a brook;   20
Or by a cyder-press, with patient look,
    Thou watchest the last oozings hours by hours.

III

Where are the songs of Spring? Ay, where are they?
  Think not of them, thou hast thy music too,—
While barred clouds bloom the soft-dying day,   25
  And touch the stubble-plains with rosy hue;
Then in a wailful choir the small gnats mourn
  Among the river sallows, borne aloft
    Or sinking as the light wind lives or dies;
And full-grown lambs loud bleat from hilly bourn; 30
  Hedge-crickets sing; and now with treble soft
  The red-breast whistles from a garden-croft;
    And gathering swallows twitter in the skies.

Ode on Melancholy

I

No, no, go not to Lethe, neither twist
  Wolf's-bane, tight-rooted, for its poisonous wine;
Nor suffer thy pale forehead to be kiss'd
  By nightshade, ruby grape of Proserpine;
Make not your rosary of yew-berries,   5
  Nor let the beetle, nor the death-moth be
    Your mournful Psyche, nor the downy owl
A partner in your sorrow's mysteries;
  For shade to shade will come too drowsily,
    And drown the wakeful anguish of the soul.   10

II

But when the melancholy fit shall fall
  Sudden from heaven like a weeping cloud,
That fosters the droop-headed flowers all,
  And hides the green hill in an April shroud;
Then glut thy sorrow on a morning rose,   15

Or on the rainbow of the salt sand-wave,
    Or on the wealth of globed peonies;
Or if thy mistress some rich anger shows,
    Emprison her soft hand, and let her rave,
        And feed deep, deep upon her peerless eyes.   20

III

She dwells with Beauty—Beauty that must die;
    And Joy, whose hand is ever at his lips
Bidding adieu; and aching Pleasure nigh,
    Turning to Poison while the bee-mouth sips:
Ay, in the very temple of delight   25
    Veil'd Melancholy had her sovran shrine,
        Though seen of none save him whose strenuous tongue
    Can burst Joy's grape against his palate fine;
His soul shall taste the sadness of her might,
    And be among her cloudy trophies hung.   30

Ode on Indolence

'They toil not, neither do they spin.'

I

ONE morn before me were three figures seen,
    With bowed necks, and joined hands, side-faced;
And one behind the other stepp'd serene,
    In placid sandals, and in white robes graced;
They pass'd, like figures on a marble urn,   5
    When shifted round to see the other side;
        They came again; as when the urn once more
Is shifted round, the first seen shades return;
    And they were strange to me, as may betide
        With vases, to one deep in Phidian lore.   10

II

How is it, Shadows! that I knew ye not?
    How came ye muffled in so hush a mask?
Was it a silent deep-disguised plot
    To steal away, and leave without a task
My idle days? Ripe was the drowsy hour;   15

The blissful cloud of summer-indolence
　　Benumb'd my eyes; my pulse grew less and less;
Pain had no sting, and pleasure's wreath no flower:
　　O, why did ye not melt, and leave my sense
　　　　Unhaunted quite of all but—nothingness?　　　20

III

A third time came they by;—alas! wherefore?
　　My sleep has been embroider'd with dim dreams;
My soul had been a lawn besprinkled o'er
　　With flowers, and stirring shades, and baffled beams.
The morn was clouded, but no shower fell,　　　25
　　Tho' in her lids hung the sweet tears of May;
　　　　The open casement press'd a new-leav'd vine,
　　Let in the budding warmth and throstle's lay;
O Shadows! 'twas a time to bid farewell!
　　　　Upon your skirts had fallen no tears of mine.　　　30

IV

A third time pass'd they by, and, passing, turn'd
　　Each one the face a moment whiles to me;
Then faded, and to follow them I burn'd
　　And ach'd for wings because I knew the three;
The first was a fair Maid, and Love her name;　　　35
　　The second was Ambition, pale of cheek,
　　　　And ever watchful with fatigued eye;
The last, whom I love more, the more of blame
　　Is heap'd upon her, maiden most unmeek,—
　　　　I knew to be my demon Poesy.　　　40

V

They faded, and, forsooth! I wanted wings:
　　O folly! What is love! and where is it?
And for that poor Ambition! it springs
　　From a man's little heart's short fever-fit;
For Poesy!—no,—she has not a joy,—　　　45
　　At least for me,—so sweet as drowsy noons,
　　　　And evenings steep'd in honied indolence;
O, for an age so shelter'd from annoy,
　　That I may never know how change the moons,
　　　　Or hear the voice of busy common-sense!　　　50

VI

So, ye Three Ghosts, adieu! Ye cannot raise
  My head cool-bedded in the flowery grass;
For I would not be dieted with praise,
  A pet-lamb in a sentimental farce!
Fade softly from my eyes, and be once more   55
  In masque-like figures on the dreamy urn;
    Farewell! I yet have visions for the night,
And for the day faint visions there is store;
    Vanish, ye Phantoms! from my idle spright,
  Into the clouds, and never more return!   60

CHAPTER TWO

THE LETTERS

Introduction

> . . . some kind of letters are good squares others handsome ovals, and other some orbicular, others spheroid—and why should there not be another species with two rough edges like a Rat-trap? I hope you will find all my long letters of that species, and all will be well; for by merely touching the spring delicately and etherially, the rough edged will fly immediately into a proper compactness; and thus you may make a good wholesome loaf, with your own leven in it, of my fragments . . .
>
> Letter 64. To John Hamilton Reynolds
Sunday 3 May 1818

T. S. Eliot observed that Keats' ". . . greatness . . . is manifested more clearly in his Letters than in his poems; and . . . seems to me to be much more the kind of Shakespeare. The Letters are certainly the most notable and the most important ever written by any English poet. . . . His observations . . . are of the finest quality of criticism, and the deepest penetration. . . . There is hardly one statement of Keats about poetry which . . . will not be found to be true . . ."[1]

The truth of these remarks even a selection from the letters should make clear. To feel their full force, and the living presence of Keats' vibrant humanity, you should read all of the letters, or at least as generous a selection as that by Frederick Page, in his *Letters of John Keats,* published by the Oxford University Press in "The World's Classics" series. It is Mr. Page's text, based on the 1952 edition of the letters by Maurice Buxton Forman, corrected and emended by Professor Hyder Rollins, which is here followed.

I have tried to include in this selection every passage from Keats'

[1] T. S. Eliot, *The Use of Poetry and The Use of Criticism* (Cambridge: Harvard University Press, 1933), pp. 91-93.

letters which because of date of composition, subject, theme, or verbal rendering seems to illuminate one's reading of the "Ode on a Grecian Urn." Keats nowhere in his letters actually mentions the Ode, but the complex of ideas with which it deals is to be found throughout them. What one can see even in a selection is the startling, almost minute by minute growth of a human being whose period of maturity was one of the shortest and richest of which we have record.

A Chronological Account of the Life of John Keats, containing brief sketches of the recipients of letters included in the selection below.

Keats has been unusually fortunate in his biographers, from Sidney Colvin to those of our own time. The slow, patient, and exact accumulation of new knowledge and the correction of older knowledge or belief about Keats, taken all in all, is one of the most impressive records of humanistic scholarship in modern times. No sketch as brief as the one in this book must be could do justice to the many complex issues of fact and interpretation involved in studying Keats' life. For that, the reader is referred to the numerous biographies from which excerpts are taken in Chapter Three, to the MacGillivray bibliography of Keats, and to the annual bibliographies in the *Publications of the Modern Language Association* and the *Keats-Shelley Journal.* For a reliable short account of Keats' life and a judicious bibliography on the subject, see Samuel C. Chew, "John Keats," in *A Literary History of England,* ed. A. C. Baugh and others (New York: Appleton-Century-Crofts, 1948), pp. 1241-1251. For the chronology below I have drawn on the 1952 edition of *The Letters of John Keats,* edited by Maurice Buxton Forman (Toronto: Oxford University Press, 1952); for the sketches, on Forman and especially on the first volume of Professor Hyder Rollins' *The Keats Circle: Letters and Papers, 1816-1878* (Cambridge: Harvard University Press, 1948).

1795	Oct. 31	Birth of John Keats.
1797	Feb. 28	Birth of his brother George.
1799	Nov. 18	Birth of his brother Thomas.
1803	June 3	Birth of his sister Fanny.
1804	April 16	Death of his father.
	June 27	Marriage of his mother to William Rawlings.
1804-1810		Living with his grandmother, Mrs. Jennings.
1810	March	Death of his mother.
1803-1811		Attending Clarke's School, Enfield.
1811	Summer	Apprenticed to Thomas Hammond, Surgeon.

1812		Writes "Imitation of Spenser."
1813		Meets Joseph Severn.
1814	Dec.	Death of his grandmother.
1815	Oct. 1	Entered at Guy's Hospital.
1816	May 5	First published poem, sonnet "O Solitude!" appears in *The Examiner*.
	July 25	Takes the Apothecaries' Society's Certificate.
		Writes first great poem, sonnet "On First Looking into Chapman's Homer."
1817	March 3	First book, *Poems,* published.
	Spring	Begins "Endymion."
	April 17-18	Letter No. 13 to John Hamilton Reynolds. See also: Letters No. 30, Nov. 22, 1817; No. 64, May 3, 1818; No. 87, Sept. 22, 1818; No. 145, August 24, 1819.

Born September 9, 1794, Reynolds died November 15, 1852. He and Keats first met no later than October, 1816, by which date he had published a number of poems. Literature, in which he was not ungifted, was his avocation; he turned to the law in November, 1817; in the "dreary profession," as he called it, he remained; more active than he was successful, in his later years especially he was somewhat more successful than he was reliable. Keats considered him one who "makes you laugh and not think." Reynolds was a good influence on Keats as a poet in a number of ways, but, perhaps because Reynolds thought poorly of Fanny Brawne, the relationship between the two men seems not as strong at the end of Keats' life as it had been earlier. His highest distinction, as Professor Rollins points out, is in the last line on his tombstone: "The friend of Keats."

| 1817 | May 10-11 | Letter No. 15 to Benjamin Robert Haydon. See also: Letter No. 115, March 8, 1819. |

Born January 26, 1786, Haydon, after an eventful and violent career as an artist, committed suicide on June 22, 1846. He was thirty-one, Keats twenty-one when they first met. At that time Haydon was famous and well-established, and he is often credited with creating Keats' enthusiasm for ancient art. He himself painted enormous historical subjects; the tragedy of his career, as Aldous Huxley points out, was that his gift was literary, not pictorial. Keats' affection for Haydon, somewhat cooled later by the latter's unwillingness to repay a debt when Keats was desperate for money, was unusually strong.

| 1817 | Oct. 30 | Letter No. 26 to Benjamin Bailey. See also: Letters No. 28, Nov. 3, 1817; No. 31, Nov. 22, 1817; No. 40, Jan. 23, 1818; No. 53, March 13, 1818. |

Born June 5, 1791, Bailey died on June 25, 1853. A devoted Words-worthian, Bailey met Keats in the spring of 1817 while a student at Oxford. Keats spent the following September at Oxford with Bailey and wrote Book III of *Endymion* there; here also the two men read and discussed Wordsworth and Milton. Keats' judgment the following January—that Bailey was "one of the noblest men alive at the present day"—was clearly excessive, as Keats himself came to see. Bailey be-came an Anglican priest in 1818, a profession with which Keats was not much impressed; and he was upset by Bailey's courtship of one young lady and marriage to another. In 1831, Bailey became Colonial Chaplain in Ceylon, and fell so out of touch with the Keats circle that Milnes, in his first edition of his life of Keats in 1848, reported Bailey dead soon after Keats.

1817	Nov. 28	Draft of "Endymion" completed.
1818	Jan. 30	Letter No. 42 to John Taylor. See also: Letters No. 51, Feb. 27, 1818; No. 62, April 24, 1818. See further: Letter No. 90 to James Augustus Hessey, Oct. 9, 1818.

Born on July 31, 1781, Taylor died on July 5, 1864; Hessey, born August 28, 1785, died on April 7, 1870. The firm of Taylor and Hessey published Keats' last two books, in 1818 and 1820. Both men helped Keats in every way, not only as publishers but as friends. Neither had any doubts as to his greatness during or after Keats' life.

1818	April 26-May 3	*Endymion* published by Taylor and Hessey
	June 22	George Keats and his bride, Georgiana, leave London for America.
	July	Tour of Scotland with Brown. Catches violent cold in Isle of Mull, with throat ulcers.
	Sept.	Begins "Hyperion." Return of sore throat. First meeting with Fanny Brawne.
	Sept. 20-21	Letter No. 86, to Charles Wentworth Dilke. See also: Letter No. 153, Sept. 22, 1819.

Born December 8, 1789, he died on August 10, 1864. He and Keats were on friendly terms sometime prior to the fall of 1817. Author and editor, he was an accurate student of literature and an opinionated student of life. Keats and his brothers and sister were all cordially treated by Dilke and his wife; the latter introduced Keats to Fanny Brawne, although they did not approve of his subsequent engagement to her. Of Dilke, Keats keenly observed: "Dilke will never come at a truth as long as he lives; because he is always trying at it."

1818	Oct. 27	Letter No. 93, to Richard Woodhouse.

Born on December 11, 1788, he died on September 3, 1834. Never an intimate friend of Keats, he was nonetheless, as Professor Rollins points out, "one of the most interesting and about the most foresighted. . . ." In spite of its faults, he recognized Keats' first major poem, *Endymion,* as the work of a genius of an order that "has not appeared since Shakespeare & Milton." Because of this opinion, Woodhouse began at once to preserve in the original or to make exact transcripts of every document by or about Keats he could; later scholars, thus, are deeply in his debt.

1818	Dec. 1	Death of Thomas Keats, nursed by John through his last illness. The relationship among the three brothers was very close, and George, the third brother, stated that there was no man who understood John as well as Tom did. In less than six months, thus, John was separated from one brother by death, and from the other by emigration.
	Dec. 25	Becomes informally engaged to Fanny Brawne.
1819	January	Writes "The Eve of St. Agnes."
	February	Persistent sore throat.
	Feb. 14-May 3	Letter No. 123, to George and Georgiana Keats.

Born February 28, 1797, George Keats died December 24, 1841. Shortly after his marriage to Georgiana Wylie, he emigrated to the United States, hoping to improve his family finances. He returned to England only once, in January, 1820. Because of the distance between them, John Keats' letters to his brother and sister-in-law are all written over periods of several days, weeks or months; in them, he took up and dropped subject after subject, since the letters are on the order of a journal or diary.

1819	April	Writes "La Belle Dame sans Merci," "Ode to Psyche," "Ode on a Grecian Urn."
	May	Writes "Ode to a Nightingale."
	June-July	Persistent sore throat.
	July	Writes Part One of "Lamia."
	July 8	Letter No. 136, to Fanny Brawne. See also: Letters No. 160, Oct. 13, 1819; No. 186, Feb. 1820; No. 205, March, 1820.

Born August 9, 1800, she died on Dec. 4, 1865. On no other person connected with Keats has contemporary and scholarly opinion varied so widely. She has been pointed to as the inspiration of his greatest poems, and as the real cause of his death. It is hard to find a common ground upon which to characterize her, but it may perhaps be said that in his love for her, Keats was more fascinated than she was fascinating. The thirty-nine letters to her from Keats are remarkable even among his letters for the intensity, the violence and the passionate alteration of mood they display; a mature and experienced woman would have found them almost too much to bear, and Fanny was only, it would appear, a fairly normal, respectably raised, girl of nineteen. Whatever her effect on his life, Keats immortalized her, nowhere more unforgettably than in the lines written in the margin of a page of the manuscript of "The Cap and Bells":

> This living hand, now warm and capable
> Of earnest grasping, would if it were cold
> And in the icy silence of the tomb,
> So haunt thy days and chill thy dreaming nights
> That thou would wish thine own heart dry of blood
> So in my veins red life might stream again,
> And thou be conscience-calm'd—see here it is—
> I hold it towards you.

Accounts of Fanny Brawne may be found in Colvin, Lowell, Murry, Gittings and other biographers and critics of Keats. See also, Joanna Richardson, *Fanny Brawne* (London: Thames and Hudson, 1952).

1819	July 25	Probably wrote the sonnet, "Bright Star."
	Sept. 5	"Lamia" finished.
	Sept. 10-15	Writes "Ode to Autumn," revises "The Eve of St. Agnes."
	Oct.-Nov.	Writing "The Cap and Bells."
	Dec.	Throat in threatening state again.
1820	January	"Ode on a Grecian Urn" published in *Annals of the Fine Arts.*
	Feb. 3	Fatal illness begins.
	June 22	Fresh attack of blood-spitting.
	July	*Lamia, Isabella, The Eve of St. Agnes, and Other Poems* published, "the greatest single volume," says Professor S. C. Chew, "of English poetry of the nineteenth century."
	Aug. 12	Returns to Hampstead to be nursed by Mrs. and Miss Brawne.
	Sept. 13	Leaves Hampstead for the last time.
	Sept. 18	Sails with Severn from Gravesend for Italy.
	Sept. 30	Letter No. 239, to Charles Armitage Brown. See also: Letters No. 241, Nov. 1, 1820; No. 242, Nov. 30, 1820.

Born in June, 1786, he died in June, 1842. Brown, says Professor Rollins, "was a strange mixture of coarseness, kindliness, coldbloodness, and calculation." Keats lived with him at Hampstead, next door to the Brawnes. During Keats' illnesses, Brown was a patient and devoted nurse to the poet, yet after Keats' death, Brown sent a bill for room and board to George Keats, who paid it. A man whose marital arrangements were at best irregular, Brown was thought by Keats to be flirting with Fanny Brawne, which led him in the summer of 1820 to write to Fanny: ". . . though I know his love and friendship for me, though at this moment I should be without pence were it not for his assistance, I will never see or speak to him until we are both old men, if we are to be."

1820	Oct. 21	Reaches Naples; detained in quarantine.
	Nov. 17(?)	Enters Rome.
	Nov. 30	Writes his last letter.
	Dec. 10	Has a serious relapse.
1821	Feb. 26	His death.

The Texts

13. To John Hamilton Reynolds, Thursday 17—Friday 18 April [*1817*]
I find that I cannot exist without poetry—without eternal poetry—half the day will not do—the whole of it—I began with a little, but habit has made me a Leviathan—I had become all in a Tremble from not having written any thing of late—the Sonnet over leaf did me some good. I slept the better last night for it—this Morning, however, I am nearly as bad again—Just now I opened Spencer, and the first Lines I saw were these.—

> "The noble Heart that harbors virtuous thought,
> And is with Child of glorious great intent,
> Can never rest, until it forth have brought
> Th' eternal Brood of Glory excellent—"[2]

15. To Benjamin Robert Haydon, Saturday & Sunday 10-11 May *1817*
However I must think that difficulties nerve the Spirit of a Man—they make our Prime Objects a Refuge as well as a Passion. The Trumpet of Fame is as a tower of Strength the ambitious bloweth it and is safe. I suppose by your telling me not to give way to forebodings George has mentioned to you what I have lately said in my Letters to him—truth is I have been in such a state of Mind as to read over my Lines and hate them. I am "one that gathers Samphire dreadful trade"[3] the Cliff of Poesy Towers above me—yet when,

[2] *Faerie Queen.* 1. V. 1-4.
[3] *King Lear.* IV. vi. 16.

Tom who meets with some of Pope's Homer in Plutarch's Lives reads some of those to me they seem like Mice[4] to mine.

26.   To Benjamin Bailey, ?29, 30 October 1817 [R.]
It is a bold thing to say and I would not say it in print—but it seems to me that if Wordsworth had thought a little deeper at that Moment he would not have written the Poem at all—I should judge it to have been written in one of the most comfortable Moods of his Life—it is a kind of sketchy intellectual Landscape—not a search after Truth . . .[5]

28.   To Benjamin Bailey, Monday 3 Nov. 1817
O for a recourse somewhat human independant of the Great Consolations of Religion and undepraved Sensations—of the Beautiful—the poetical in all things—O for a Remedy against such wrongs within the pale of the World! Should not those things be pure enjoyment should they stand the chance of being contaminated by being called in as antagonists to Bishops? Would not earthly thing do? By Heavens my dear Bailey I know you have a spice of what I mean . . .

30.   To John Hamilton Reynolds, Saturday 22 Nov. 1817
Why don't you, as I do, look unconcerned at what may be called more particularly Heart-vexations? They never surprize me—lord! a man should have the fine point of his soul taken off to become fit for this world—I like this place very much. . . . One of the three Books I have with me is Shakespear's Poems: I neer found so many beauties in the Sonnets[6]—they seem to be full of fine things said unintentionally—in the intensity of working out conceits.

31.   To Benjamin Bailey, Saturday 22 Nov. 1817
In passing however I must say of one thing that has pressed upon me lately and encreased my Humility and capability of submission and that is this truth—Men of Genius are great as certain ethereal Chemicals operating on the Mass of neutral intellect—by [*for* but] they have not any individuality, any determined Character. . . . O I wish I was as certain of the end of all your troubles as that of your momentary start about the authenticity of the Imagination. I am certain of nothing but of the holiness of the Heart's affections and the truth of Imagination—What the imagination seizes as Beauty must be truth—whether it existed before or not—for I have the same Idea of all our Passions as of Love they are all in their sublime, creative of essential Beauty. . . . The Imagination may be compared to Adam's

4 *Ibid.* IV. vi. 19.
5 Cf. Wordsworth, "Gipsies." [L.]
6 Respectively xii, xvii, xix, xxi, xiii,

dream[7]—he awoke and found it truth. I am the more zealous in this affair, because I have never yet been able to perceive how any thing can be known for truth by consequitive reasoning—and yet it must be. Can it be that even the greatest Philosopher ever arrived at his goal without putting aside numerous objections. However it may be, O for a Life of Sensations rather than of Thoughts! It is 'a Vision in the form of Youth' a Shadow of reality to come—and this consideration has further convinced me for it has come as auxiliary to another favorite Speculation of mine, that we shall enjoy ourselves here after by having what we called happiness on Earth repeated in a finer tone and so repeated. And yet such a fate can only befall those who delight in Sensation rather than hunger as you do after Truth. Adam's dream will do here and seems to be a conviction that Imagination and its empyreal reflection is the same as human Life and its Spiritual repetition. But as I was saying—the simple imaginative Mind may have its rewards in the repeti[ti]on of its own silent Working coming continually on the Spirit with a fine Suddenness— to compare great things with small—have you never by being Surprised with an old Melody—in a delicious place—by a delicious voice, fe[l]t over again your very Speculations and Surmises at the time it first operated on your Soul—do you not remember forming to yourself the singer's face more beautiful that [*for* than] it was possible and yet with the elevation of the Moment you did not think so— even then you were mounted on the Wings of Imagination so high— that the Prototype must be here after that delicious face you will see. . . . You perhaps at once time thought there was such a thing as Worldly Happiness to be arrived at, at certain periods of time marked out—you have of necessity from your disposition been thus led away—I scarcely remember counting upon any Happiness—I look not for it if it be not in the present hour—nothing startles me beyond the Moment. The setting Sun will always set me to rights—or if a Sparrow come before my Window I take part in its existince and pick about the Gravel.

32.   To George and Thomas Keats, Sunday 21 Dec. 1817 [perhaps finished after 26 Dec. R.]
I spent Friday evening with Wells,[8] and went the next morning to see *Death on the Pale Horse*.[9] It is a wonderful picture, when West's age is considered; But there is nothing to be intense upon; no women one feels mad to kiss; no face swelling into reality—the excellence

---

[7] See *Paradise Lost*, viii. 460-90.
[8] Charles Wells (1800-79), the author of "Stories after Nature" and "Joseph and his Brethern."
[9] By Benjamin West, P. R. A. (1738-1820). "Christ rejected" was also by West.

of every Art is its intensity, capable of making all disagreeables evaporate, from their being in close relationship with Beauty and Truth—Examine King Lear and you will find this exemplified throughout; but in this picture we have unpleasantness without any momentous depth of speculation excited, in which to bury its repulsiveness. . . . [S]everal things dovetailed in my mind, and at once it struck me what quality went to form a Man of Achievement especially in Literature and which Shakespeare possessed so enormously— I mean *Negative Capability,* that is when man is capable of being in uncertainties, Mysteries, doubts, without any irritable reaching after fact and reason—Coleridge, for instance, would let go by a fine isolated verisimilitude caught from the Penetralium of mystery, from being incapable of remaining Content with half knowledge. This pursued through Volumes would perhaps take us no further than this, that with a great poet the sense of Beauty overcomes every other consideration, or rather obliterates all consideration.

42.   To John Taylor, Friday 30 Jan. 1818
   These Lines, as they now stand, about Happiness have rung in my ears like a 'chime a mending'.[10] See, here,
                              Behold
           Wherein Lies happiness Pœona? fold—
This appears to me the very contrary of blessed. I hope this will appear to you more elegible.
           Wherein lies Happiness? In that which becks
           Our ready Minds to fellowship divine;
           A fellowship with essence, till we shine
           Full alchymized and free of space. Behold
           The clear Religion of heaven—fold. &c—
You must indulge me by putting this in for setting aside the badness of the other, such a preface is necessary to the subject. The whole thing must I think have appeared to you, who are a consequitive Man, as a thing almost of mere words—but I assure you that when I wrote it it was a regular stepping of the Imagination towards a Truth. My having written that ~~Passage~~ Argument will perhaps be of the greatest Service to me of any thing I ever did. It set before me at once the gradations of Happiness even like a kind of Pleasure Thermometer—and is my first Step towards the chief attempt in the Drama—the playing of different Natures with Joy and Sorrow.

51.   To John Taylor, Friday 27 Feb. 1818
   Your alteration strikes me as being a great improvement—the page looks much better. And now I will attend to the Punctuations you

10 *Troilus and Cressida,* I. iii. 159.

speak of—the comma should be at *soberly*,[11] and in the other passage
the comma should follow *quiet*,[12]. I am extremely indebted to you
for this attention and also for your after admonitions—It is a sorry
thing for me that any one should have to overcome Prejudices in
reading my Verses—that affects me more than any hypercriticism on
any particular Passage. In *Endymion* I have most likely but moved
into the Go-cart from the leading strings. In Poetry I have a few
Axioms, and you will see how far I am from their Centre. 1st. I think
Poetry should surprise by a fine excess and not by Singularity—it
should strike the Reader as a wording of his own highest thoughts,
and appear almost a Remembrance—2nd. Its touches of Beauty
should never be half way ther[e] by making the reader breathless
instead of content: the rise, the progress, the setting of imagery
should like the Sun come natural natural too him—shine over him
and set soberly although in magnificence leaving him in the Luxury
of twilight—but it is easier to think what Poetry should be than to
write it—and this leads me on to another axiom. That if Poetry
comes not as naturally as the Leaves to a tree it had better not come
at all. However it may be with me I cannot help looking into new
countries with 'O for a Muse of fire to ascend!'[13]

53.   *To Benjamin Bailey, Friday [13 March 1818]*

I am sometimes so very sceptical as to think Poetry itself a mere
Jack a lanthen to amuse whoever may chance to be struck with its
brilliance. As Tradesmen say everything is worth what it will fetch,
so probably every mental pursuit takes its reality and worth from
the ardour of the pursuer—being in itself a nothing—Ethereal thing[s]
may at least be thus real, divided under three heads—Things real—
things semireal—and no things. Things real—such as existences of
Sun Moon & Stars and passages of Shakespeare. Things semireal such
as Love, the Clouds &c which require a greeting of the Spirit to make
them wholly exist—and Nothings which are made Great and digni-
fied by an ardent pursuit—which by the by stamps the burgundy
mark on the bottles of our Minds, insomuch as they are able to
"consec[r]ate whate'er they look upon".[14]

62.   *To John Taylor, Friday 24 April 1818*

I know nothing I have read nothing and I mean to follow Solomon's
directions of 'get Wisdom—get understanding'[15]—I find cavalier days
are gone by. I find that I can have no enjoyment in the World but

11 "Endymion," i. 149.
12 *Ibid.*, i. 247.
13 *Henry V*, Prologue I.
14 Cf Shelley, "Hymn to Intellectual Beauty," st. 2.
15 *Proverbs* iv. 5.

continual drinking of Knowledge—I find there is no worthy pursuit but the idea of doing some good for the world . . . there is but one way for me—the road lies th[r]ough application study and thought. . . . I have been hovering for some time between an exquisite sense of the luxurious and a love for Philosophy—were I calculated for the former I should be glad—but as I am not I shall turn all my soul to the latter.

64.   To John Hamilton Reynolds, Sunday 3 May 1818
Were I to study physic or rather Medicine again, I feel it would not make the least difference in my Poetry; when the Mind is in its infancy a Bias is in reality a Bias, but when we have acquired more strength, a Bias becomes no Bias. Every department of Knowledge we see excellent and calculated towards a great whole. I am so convinced of this, that I am glad at not having given away my medical Books, which I shall again look over to keep alive the little I know thitherwards; and moreover intend through you and Rice to become a sort of pip-civilian. An extensive knowledge is needful to thinking people—it takes away the heat and fever; and helps, by widening speculation, to ease the Burden of the Mystery:[16] a thing I begin to understand a little, and which weighed upon you in the most gloomy and true sentence in your Letter. The difference of high Sensations with and without knowledge appears to me this—in the latter case we are falling continually ten thousand fathoms deep and being blown up again without wings and with all [the] horror of a bare shouldered creature—in the former case, our shoulders are fledge, and we go thro' the same air and space without fear. . . .

86.   To Charles Wentworth Dilke, 20 and 21 Sept. 1818 [R.]
I wish I could say Tom was any better. His identity presses upon me so all day that I am obliged to go out—and although I intended to have given some time to study alone I am obliged to write, and plunge into abstract images to ease myself of his countenance his voice and feebleness—so that I live now in a continual fever—it must be poisonous to life although I feel well. Imagine 'the hateful siege of contraries.'[17]—if I think of fame of poetry it seems a crime to me, and yet I must do so or suffer—I am sorry to give you pain—I am almost resolv'd to burn this—but I really have not self possession and magninimity enough to manage the thing otherwise . . .

87.   To John Hamilton Reynolds, [Tuesday 22 Sept. 1818?]
I never was in love—yet the voice and the shape of a Woman has

16 Wordsworth, "Tintern Abbey," l. 38.
17 *Paradise Lost,* IX. 121, 122.

haunted me these two days—at such a time when the relief, the feverous relief of Poetry seems a much less crime—This morning Poetry has conquered—I have relapsed into those abstractions which are my only life—I feel escaped from a new strange and threatening sorrow.—and I am thankful for it.—There is an awful warmth about my heart like a load of Immortality.

Poor Tom—that woman—and Poetry were ringing changes in my senses.—Now I am in comparison happy—I am sensible this will distress you—you must forgive me.

90.   To James Augustus Hessey, Friday 9 Oct. 1818
Praise or blame has but a momentary effect on the man whose love of beauty in the abstract makes him a severe critic on his own Works. My own domestic criticism has given me pain without comparison beyond what Blackwood or the Quarterly could possibly inflict . . . J. S. is perfectly right in regard to the slip-shod Endymion . . . Had I been nervous about it being a perfect piece, & with that view asked advice, & trembled over every page, it would not have been written; for it is not in my nature to fumble—I will write independantly.—I have written independently *without Judgment.*—I may write independently, & *with Judgment* hereafter. The Genius of Poetry must work out its own salvation in a man: It cannot be matured by law and precept, but by sensation & watchfulness in itself. That which is creative must create itself—In Endymion, I leaped headlong into the Sea, and thereby have become better acquainted with the Soundings, the quicksands, & the rocks, than if I had stayed upon the green shore, and piped a silly pipe, and took tea & comfortable advice.—I was never afraid of failure; for I would sooner fail than not be among the greatest.

93.   To Richard Woodhouse, Tuesday 27 Oct. 1818
1st. As to the poetical Character itself (I mean that sort of which, if I am any thing, I am a Member; that sort distinguished from the wordsworthian or egotistical sublime; which is a thing per se and stands alone) it is not itself—it has no self—it is everything and nothing—It has no character—it enjoys light and shade; it lives in gusto, be it foul or fair, high or low, rich or poor, mean or elevated—It has as much delight in conceiving an Iago as an Imogen. What shocks the virtuous philosopher, delights the camelion Poet. It does no harm from its relish of the dark side of things any more than from its taste for the bright one; because they both end in speculation. . . . It is a wretched thing to confess; but is a very fact that not one word I ever utter can be taken for granted as an opinion growing out of my identical nature—how can it, when I have no nature? When I am in a room with People if I ever am free from speculating on creations

of my own brain, then not myself goes home to myself: but the identity of every one in the room begins to [*for* so] to press upon me that I am in a very little time an[ni]hilated—not only among Men; it would be the same in a Nursery of children . . .

In the second place I will speak of my views, and of the life I purpose to myself. I am ambitious of doing the world some good: if I should be spared that may be the work of maturer years—in the interval I will assay to reach to as high a summit in Poetry as the nerve bestowed upon me will suffer. The faint conceptions I have of Poems to come brings the blood frequently into my forehead. All I hope is that I may not lose all interest in human affairs—that the solitary indifference I feel for applause even from the finest Spirits, will not blunt any acuteness of vision I may have. I do not think it will—I feel assured I should write from the mere yearning and fondness I have for the Beautiful even if my night's labours should be burnt every morning, and no eye ever shine upon them. But even now I am perhaps not speaking from myself; but from some character in whose soul I now live.

115. To Benjamin Robert Haydon, Monday 8 March 1819
With respect to my livelihood, I will not write for it,—for I will not run with that most vulgar of all crowds, the literary. Such things I ratify by looking upon myself, and trying myself at lifting mental weights, as it were. I am three and twenty, with little knowle[d]ge and middling intellect. It is true that in the height of enthusiasm I have been cheated into some fine passages; but that is not the thing.

123. To George and Georgiana Keats, Sunday 14 Feb.—Monday 3 May 1819
A Man's life of any worth is a continual allegory—and very few eyes can see the Mystery of his life—a life like the scriptures, figurative— which such people can no more make out than they can the hebrew Bible. Lord Byron cuts a figure—but he is not figurative—Shakspeare led a life of Allegory: his works are the comments on it— . . .

.   .   .   .

This morning I am in a sort of temper indolent and supremely careless: I long after a stanza or two of Thompson's Castle of indolence. My passions are all asleep from my having slumbered till nearly eleven and weakened the animal fibre all over me to a delightful sensation about three degrees on this side of faintness—if I had teeth of pearl and the breath of lillies I should call it langour—but as I am* I must call it Laziness. In this state of effeminacy the fibres of the brain are relaxed in common with the rest of the body, and to

* Especially as I have a black eye. [Received playing cricket. L.]

such a happy degree that pleasure has no show of enticement and pain no unbearable frown. Neither Poetry, nor Ambition, nor Love have any alertness of countenance as they pass by me: they seem rather like three figures on a greek vase—a Man and two women whom no one but myself could distinguish in their disguisement.[18] This is the only happiness; and is a rare instance of advantage in the body overpowering the Mind. I have this moment received a note from Haslam in which he expects the death of his Father— . . . Very few men have ever arrived at a complete disinterestedness of Mind: very few have been influenced by a pure desire of the benefit of others—in the greater part of the Benefactors to Humanity some meretricious motive has sullied their greatness— . . . From the manner in which I feel Haslam's misfortune I perceive how far I am from any humble standard of disinterestedness—Yet this feeling ought to be carried to its highest pitch as there is no fear of its ever injuring Society—which it would do I fear pushed to an extremity—For in wild nature the Hawk would loose his Breakfast of Robins and the Robin his of Worms—the Lion must starve as well as the swallow. The greater part of Men make their way with the same instinctiveness, the same unwandering eye from their purposes, the same animal eagerness as the Hawk. The Hawk wants a Mate, so does the man—look at them both they set about it and procure on[e] in the same manner. They want both a nest and they both set about one in the same manner—they get their food in the same manner—The noble animal Man for his amusement smokes his pipe—the Hawk balances about the Clouds—that is the only difference of their leisures. This it is that makes the Amusement of Life— to a speculative Mind. I go among the Fields and catch a glimpse of a Stoat or a fieldmouse peeping out of the withered grass—the creature hath a purpose and its eyes are bright with it. I go amongst the buildings of a city and I see a Man hurrying along—to what? the Creature has a purpose and his eyes are bright with it. But then, as Wordsworth says, "we have all one human heart."[19]—there is an ellectric fire in human creature[s] there is continu[a]lly some birth of new heroism. The pity is that we must wonder at it: as we should at finding a pearl in rubbish. I have no doubt that thousands of people never heard of have had hearts comp[l]etely disinterested: I can remember but two—Socrates and Jesus—their Histories evince it. What I heard a little time ago, Taylor observe with respect to Socrates may be said of Jesus—That he was so great a man that though he transmitted no writing of his own to posterity, we have his Mind and his sayings and his greatness handed to us by others. It is to be lamented that the history of the latter was written and

[18] Compare the "Ode on Indolence."
[19] "The Old Cumberland Beggar," I. 153.

revised by Men interested in the pious frauds of Religion. Yet through all this I see his splendour. Even here though I myself am pursueing the same instinctive course as the veriest human animal you can think of—I am however young writing at random—straining at particles of light in the midst of a great darkness—without knowing the bearing of any one assertion of any one opinion. Yet may I not in this be free from sin? May there not be superior beings amused with any graceful, though instinctive attitude my mind m[a]y fall into, as I am entertained with the alertness of a Stoat or the anxiety of a Deer? Though a quarrel in the Streets is a thing to be hated, the energies displayed in it are fine—This is the very thing in which consists poetry; and if so it is not so fine a thing as philosophy—For the same reason that an eagle is not so fine a thing as a truth—Give me this credit—Do you not think I strive—to know myself?

.   .   .   .

This point I sincerely wish to consider because I think it a grander system of salvation than the chrystiain religion—or rather it is a system of Spirit-creation—This is effected by three grand materials acting the one upon the other for a series of years. These three Materials are the *Intelligence*—the *human heart* (as distinguished from intelligence or Mind) and the *World* or *Elemental* space suited for the proper action of *Mind and Heart* on each other for the purpose of forming the *Soul* or *Intelligence destined to possess the sense of Identity*. I can scarcely express what I but dimly perceive—and yet I think I perceive it—that you may judge the more clearly I will put it in the most homely form possible—I will call the *world* a School instituted for the purpose of teaching little children to read—I will call the *human heart* the *horn Book* used in that School—and I will call the *Child able to read, the Soul* made from that *School* and its *hornbook*. Do you not see how necessary a World of Pains and troubles is to school an Intelligence and make it a Soul? . . . Not merely is the Heart a Hornhook, It is the Minds Bible, it is the Minds experience, it is the teat from which the Mind or intelligence sucks its identity. As various as the Lives of Men are—so various become their Souls, and thus does God make individual beings, Souls, Identical Souls of the Sparks of his own essence—This appears to me a faint Sketch of a system of Salvation which does not affront our reason and humanity—I am convinced that many difficulties which christians labour under would vanish before it— . . . If what I have said should not be plain enough, as I fear it may not be, I will but [*for* put] you in the place where I began in this series of thoughts —I mean, I began by seeing how man was formed by circumstances— and what are circumstances?—but touchstones of his heart—? and

what are touchstones? but proovings of his heart? and what are
proovings of his heart but fortifiers or alterers of his nature? and
what is his altered nature but his Soul?—and what was his Soul
before it came into the world and had these provings and alterations
and perfectionings?—An intelligence—without Identity—and how is
this Identity to be made? Through the medium of the Heart? And
how is the heart to become this Medium but in a world of Circumstances? There now I think what with Poetry and Theology you may
thank your Stars that my pen is not very long winded— . . .

Brown has been here rummaging up some of my old sins—that is
to say sonnets. I do not think you remember them, so I will copy
them out as well as two or three lately written— . . . The following
Poem—[Ode to Psyche {L.}] the last I have written is the first and the
only one with which I have taken even moderate pains. I have for
the most part dash'd of[f] my lines in a hurry. This I have done
leisurely—I think it reads the more richly for it and will I hope
encourage me to write other thing[s] in even a more peac[e]able and
healthy spirit. . . .

.   .   .   .

I have been endeavouring to discover a better Sonnet Stanza than
we have. The legitimate does not suit the language over-well from
the pouncing rhymes—the other kind appears too elegiac—and the
couplet at the end of it has seldom a pleasing effect—I do not pretend
to have succeeded—it will explain itself— . . .

136.   To Fanny Brawne, Thursday 8 July 1819
All my thoughts, my unhappiest days and nights have I find not at
all cured me of my love of Beauty, but made it so intense that I am
miserable that you are not with me: or rather breathe in that dull
sort of patience that cannot be called Life. I never knew before,
what such a love as you have made me feel, was; I did not believe in
it; my Fancy was affraid of it, lest it should burn me up. But if you
will fully love me, though there may be some fire, 'twill not be more
than we can bear when moistened and bedewed with Pleasures. . . .
Why may I not speak of your Beauty, since without that I could
never have lov'd you. I cannot conceive any beginning of such love
as I have for you but Beauty. There may be a sort of love for which,
without the least sneer at it, I have the highest respect and can
admire it in others: but it has not the richness, the bloom, the full
form, the enchantment of love after my own heart. So let me speak
of you[r] Beauty, though to my own endangering; if you could be
so cruel to me as to try elsewhere its Power. You say you are affraid
I shall think you do not love me—in saying this you make me ache

the more to be near you. I am at the diligent use of my faculties here, I do not pass a day without sprawling some blank verse or tagging some rhymes; and here I must confess, that, (since I am on that subject,) I love you the more in that I believe you have liked me for my own sake and for nothing else. I have met with women whom I really think would like to be married to a Poem and to be given away by a Novel.

145. To John Hamilton Reynolds, Tuesday 24 Aug. 1819
I have nothing to speak of but myself—and what can I say but what I feel? If you should have any reason to regret this state of excitement in me, I will turn the tide of your feelings in the right channel by mentioning that it is the only state for the best sort of Poetry— that is all I care for, all I live for.

153. To Charles Wentworth Dilke, Wednesday 22 Sept. 1819
I have no trust whatever on Poetry. I dont wonder at it—the ma[r]vel it [*for* is] to me how people read so much of it. . . . Talking of Pleasure, this moment I was writing with one hand, and with the other holding to my Mouth a Nectarine—good god how fine. It went down soft pulpy, slushy, oozy—all its delicious embonpoint melted down my throat like a large beatified Strawberry.

160. To Fanny Brawne, Wednesday 13 Oct. 1819
You have absorb'd me. I have a sensation at the present moment as though I was dissolving—I should be exquisitely miserable without the hope of soon seeing you. . . . I have been astonished that Men could die Martyrs for religion—I have shudder'd at it. I shudder no more—I could be martyr'd for my Religion—Love is my religion—I could die for that. I could die for you. My Creed is Love and you are its only tenet. You have ravish'd me away by a Power I cannot resist; and yet I could resist till I saw you; and even since I have seen you I have endeavoured often 'to reason against the reasons of my Love'.[20] I can do that no more—the pain would be too great. My love is selfish. I cannot breathe without you.

186. To Fanny Brawne, [Feb. 1820?]
My sweet creature when I look back upon the pains and torments I have suffer'd for you from the day I left you to go to the isle of Wight; the extasies in which I have pass'd some days and the miseries in their turn, I wonder the more at the Beauty which has kept up the spell so fervently. . . . How illness stands as a barrier betwixt me and you! Even if I was well—I must make myself as good a Philosopher as possible. Now I have had opportunities of passing nights

20 Ford's " 'Tis Pity she's a Whore," I. iii.

anxious and awake I have found other thoughts intrude upon me. "If I should die," said I to myself, "I have left no immortal work behind me—nothing to make my friends proud of my memory—but I have lov'd the principle of beauty in all things, and if I had had time I would have made myself remember'd."

205.   *To Fanny Brawne, [March 1820?]*

I fear I am too prudent for a dying kind of Lover. Yet, there is a great difference between going off in warm blood like Romeo, and making one's exit like a frog in a frost . . .

223.   *To Fanny Brawne, [May or June 1820 [R.]]*

I long to believe in immortality. I shall never be able to bid you an entire farewell. If I am destined to be happy with you here—how short is the longest Life. I wish to believe in immortality—I wish to live with you for ever.

227.   *To Percy Bysshe Shelley, 16 Aug. 1820*

I received a copy of the Cenci, as from yourself from Hunt. There is only one part of it I am judge of; the Poetry, and dramatic effect, which by many spirits now a days is considered the mammon. . . . You I am sure will forgive me for sincerely remarking that you might curb your magnanimity and be more of an artist, and 'load every rift' of your subject with ore.[21] The thought of such discipline must fall like cold chains upon you, who perhaps never sat with your wings furl'd for six Months together. And is not this extraordinary talk for the writer of Endymion! whose mind was like a pack of scattered cards—I am picked up and sorted to a pip. My Imagination is a Monastry and I am its Monk—you must explain my metapes to yourself.

239.   *To Charles Brown, Saturday 30 Sept. 1820*

I wish for death every day and night to deliver me from these pains, and then I wish death away, for death would destroy even those pains which are better than nothing. Land and Sea, weakness and decline are great seperators, but death is the great divorcer for ever. When the pang of this thought has passed through my mind, I may say the bitterness of death is passed. . . . The thought of leaving Miss Brawne is beyond everything horrible—the sense of darkness coming over me—I eternally see her figure eternally vanishing. Some of the phrases she was in the habit of using during my last nursing at Wentworth place ring in my ears. Is there another Life? Shall I awake and find all this a dream? There must be we cannot be created for this sort of suffering.

21 Cf. Spenser, *Faerie Queene*, II. vii. 28, I. 5.

241.   To Charles Brown, Wednesday 1 Nov. 1820
The persuasion that I shall see her no more will kill me. I cannot
q— My dear Brown, I should have had her when I was in health,
and I should have remained well. I can bear to die—I cannot bear to
leave her. Oh, God! God! God! Every thing I have in my trunks that
reminds me of her goes through me like a spear. The silk lining she
put in my travelling cap scalds my head. My imagination is horribly
vivid about her—I see her—I hear her. There is nothing in the world
of sufficient interest to divert me from her a moment. . . . Where
can I look for consolation or ease? If I had any chance of recovery,
this passion would kill me. . . .

242.   To Charles Brown, Thursday 30 Nov. 1820
There is one thought enough to kill me—I have been well, healthy,
alert &c, walking with her—and now—the knowledge of contrast,
feeling for light and shade, all that information (primitive sense)
necessary for a poem are great enemies to the recovery of the stomach.
There, you rogue, I put you to the torture,—but you must bring your
philosophy to bear—as I do mine, really—or how should I be able to
live? . . . Write to George as soon as you receive this, and tell him
how I am, as far as you can guess;—and also a note to my sister—who
walks about my imagination like a ghost—she is so like Tom. I can
scarcely bid you good bye even in a letter. I always made an
awkward bow.

God bless you!

John Keats.

CHAPTER THREE

... AND THE COMMENTATORS

Introduction
Criticism: What It Is and What It Does

Since, to paraphrase Heraclitus, the same critic or reader can never read the same poem twice, criticism, like any attempt at understanding, is a complex business. Perhaps the best way to indicate how to use the material gathered here is to try to make a few observations about the nature and uses of criticism. In his essay "T. H. Huxley as a Literary Man," Aldous Huxley divides his famous grandfather's works into three groups and illustrates the division by posing a problem:

> To describe with precision even the simplest object is extremely difficult. Just how difficult only those who have attempted the task professionally can realize. Let me ask you to imagine yourselves suddenly called upon to explain to some Martian visitor the exact form, function and mode of operation of, say, a corkscrew. The thing seems simple enough; and yet I suspect that, after a few minutes of stammering hesitations, most of us would find ourselves reduced to making spiral gestures with a forefinger and going through a pantomime of bottle-opening.

How, after all, would you go about this task? Note first of all that Huxley does not merely say that you are called upon to describe a corkscrew; he states the problem far more clearly: "to some Martian visitor the exact form, function and mode of operation of, say, a corkscrew." And because he states the problem more clearly, we are better equipped to render an answer. This is one of the functions of literary criticism—not only to answer questions, but to discover which ones to ask, and how to ask them. If you tried to give the description called for, the wrong place to start would be with a mental picture of "what a corkscrew looks like." The right place would be with the decision as to what purpose your description was to serve, that is to say, with a decision concerning relevance. If you reflect on it for a moment, you will see that there are many different accurate ways to describe the object set before us—and that some of these ways would fail to satisfy the situation. For example, here are a few of the organizing questions on any one of which you could base your statement:

1) what does a corkscrew look like, or, what doesn't it look like. If you were trying to describe the corkscrew to a Martian, this would not be a good place to start because you and the Martian would not share any common experience of objects in our world to which you could compare the corkscrew.

2) what is it made of? This would give you a general and orderly beginning, but no more. A Martian would not be very much better off if he knew, for example, that it was made of wood and steel. But if you were addressing someone who had seen a corkscrew before, you could start with this question.

3) who uses it, or, who does not use it?

4) when is it used?

5) what does it do?

All of these questions attempt to tell what the object is by answering what it does, yet the questions differ among themselves, and would be answered very differently—though with equal accuracy—by a drunk, a moderate drinker, and an outspoken proponent of prohibition. If, in fact, you referred to a corkscrew as, say, the devil's tail, you wouldn't be describing what it looked like at all, but your auditor or reader would know what you thought of it, and for what purpose you thought, generally, it was used.

Huxley concludes the paragraph we began with this way:

> The difficulties of describing in a clear and intelligible way such an incomparably more elaborate piece of machinery than a corkscrew as a living organism, for example, are proportionately greater.

A poem may be described as a special kind of living organism, and the task of describing it—at any level—is not an easy one to do well. For the varieties of relevant description go far beyond those involved in talking of a corkscrew, and the number of significant statements which can be made within each variety is proportionately greater. Our business now is to find out about these varieties and statements, and we may well begin in much the same way we began with the corkscrew.

You may regard any statement made to you as an answer to a question, asked or unasked. In fact, one of the ways to discover what kind of a statement a remark is, or, indeed, whether it is a statement at all, is to formulate the question implied by the statement. Thus, for example, the simple statement "It's a nice day," can be said to be the answer to the question, "What is the weather like today?" But it may also be an answer to the question, "How do you feel about the weather today?" And, further, it may also be the answer to the question, "Do you want to talk about something important or do you want to keep the conversation trivial?" You will understand which question is involved from the context in which the answer is given. If a friend of yours walked out of a tough exam, threw his hands up in the air, and said, "Well, it's a nice day," you'd know he wasn't talking about the weather, and also that he'd answered the question, "How did you do on the exam?" If, on the other hand, the remark was made to you as you eased yourself into the barber's chair, you would understand a different question behind it.

Literary critics and scholars, among other purposes, undertake a double function: in the first place, they try to answer all (or most of) the questions a reader must or should ask in order to understand what he is reading; in the second place, they try to formulate (and to answer) some at least of the questions the reader cannot ask. The art of asking questions, generally speaking, requires greater gifts than that of answering them. Any question, in a sense, provides part of its own answer. If you have ever taken an examination in which you were told to make up your own questions and then to answer them, you know how much more difficult it is than an ordinary exam. That is because you must make all the decisions yourself, you must decide what is and what is not important or relevant.

In general, the first function of the critic is most usually performed in book reviews: the reviewer tells you who wrote the book, what it's about, what sorts of characters are in it, where it takes place, how long it is, how much it costs, whether he thinks it is worth the price and time. But if you already own and have read a given piece of work, none of these questions is very important to you; you know these answers, the question is, where do we go from here? When you have heard someone discuss something about which you "know," whether it be a poem or a football game, and you say that you are amazed at how much more he "got out" of it, or how much he "saw" or you "missed," you are saying, in one way, that he was able to ask questions which didn't occur to you, in short, that he saw possibilities in the subject that escaped you.

The functions of the reader of poetry and criticism are similar to those of the critic and scholar. He must discover what questions the critic's statements may be said to answer, and what questions go a-begging. For instance, if a critic merely says that a given poem is the most beautiful poem ever written, he is answering, among others, these two questions, and answering "yes" to both of them: can we assume that the meaning of the word "beautiful" is understood in the same sense by reader and writer; is beauty the most important part of any poem? You can see that a simple answer of yes to both questions does not get you very far, that the critic is assuming too much, and therefore saying too little. You cannot demand of a critic that he answer all and only the questions in which you are interested, but you can make other demands.

For you can decide whether the questions the critic answers are the right ones and whether they have been properly answered; you can test the relevance and then the consistency of what the critic tells you. If, for example, he undertakes to tell you why a certain poem is beautiful, and then discusses only sources and parallels, he is not doing a good job. This has nothing to do with the relative importance of judgments as to beauty as against source-hunting; either can be done well or badly; either one can be used as part of the final rendering of the other; but one cannot be offered as the other. In this book you will see examples of criticism spoiled because the critic thought he was talking about one thing, and actually was talking about something else.

Let me give an example of how a poem may be read through a single critical concept—and of the limitations of using only one approach. Keats' first great poem was "On First Looking into Chapman's Homer." This is a poem nearly all readers consider perfect, or as nearly perfect as one can demand. The poem is a Petrarchan sonnet, which means that it has a definable abstract form: it must have a certain number of lines; the rhymes must be of a certain number and order; the divisions of thought and development in the poem must come at certain points. These things must be done no matter who writes the poem or what he writes it about if it is to be a Petrarchan sonnet. It is as a conventional form, then, that we might examine the poem, pursuing those questions which center on the idea of convention, on usages based on common practice and agreement, on what meaning is given or withheld through the interplay of convention and expectation. The form, the theme, the subject all make certain demands: words have a number of meanings, the exact one or ones being given by the context, by the way the word is used. In a perfect sonnet, all of the demands, all of the meanings, must be perfectly blended; nothing must be sacrificed in order to help something else. To put it positively, every part must sustain and enrich every other part.

We would, then, examine every word, its location, its meanings, the purposes it serves. We would discover that the key word is in the first line—"travell'd;" that the complex of ideas built around it—exploration, discovery, royal privilege and obligation, conquest—is elaborated throughout the sonnet, and is combined with two further ideas:

1) that this complex can be applied to the experience of reading a translation of Homer; which is to say, the idea of style; and

2) that this complex and the idea of style can best be combined and expressed through the Petrarchan sonnet; which is to say, the idea of form.

We would observe in particular how the necessary development of subject and the demands of the form are made to come together perfectly at every point, so that the form itself is a part of the subject, and the subject elucidates the form. Such an analysis would be extremely detailed and extremely fruitful; one of the simplest standards of excellence in a poem is this: no matter how well you know the poem, no matter how carefully you examine it, you continually find things in it you had not seen before; it always remains serenely superior to even the most delicate and loving analysis.

But there is something else we would discover which may be more important—no single critical method, no matter how thoroughly pursued, no matter how dexterously used, can answer every question. Only a combination of methods, achieved by studying, for instance, the variety of materials in this chapter, can even begin to answer many of the most significant questions. Consider, for example, the questions to which the above method of analysis would give no answers at all. One group comes immediately to mind: from making an analysis on the basis outlined above, you could form no idea of when Keats lived (except that it was sometime after Chapman); how old he was when he wrote the poem; where it comes in his career; whether it is typical of his work; what he was doing just before he wrote it; under what circumstances it was written; what sorts of materials, in books and other places, he drew on; how he shaped these materials; whether he wrote the poem straight off; whether, if he did not, we know anything about his revisions; whether they throw any light on what he was trying to reach in this poem; whether there is any evidence to indicate that he knew it was not Cortez who first looked down on the Pacific, and, if he did know, why he used Cortez; whether Homer was a passing fancy or a continuing influence in Keats' life; whether, finally, the answers to any or all of these questions would deepen or retard your understanding of the poem. It is to the last of these questions that this book is directed; it undertakes to give you a wide enough experience in critical and scholarly method on a single poem to enable you to answer that question for yourself. You will find that by combining the insights of a number of methods you can reach a richer and fuller understanding not only of the poem, but of the process of understanding and appreciation itself.

For this chapter offers some material which is brilliant, and some which is exasperating; some profound, some faked. It offers for examination what the patient accretion of knowledge can provide for the better understanding of a given piece of work. Some of the oppositions may seem (and may be) bewildering. But from these ideas (and methods and presuppositions) in conflict and complement should come a judgment which can stand attack. The ability to discriminate the good from the shoddy which, ideally, education and maturity combine to offer you is basic to every field of study; the materials gathered here, it is hoped, will help to sharpen that ability.

The Texts

No. 1 Lord Byron. H. Buxton Forman and Maurice Buxton Forman, *The Poetical Works and Other Writings of John Keats* (New York: Charles Scribner's Sons, 1937), III, 154-155n.

Although Byron allowed himself the most abominable license in writing about Keats, he does not seem to have been above appropriating his victim's thought. Stanza LXI of the Fourth Canto of *Don Juan* reads thus:—

> The ruling passion, such as marble shows
>   When exquisitely chisell'd, still lay there,
> But fix'd as marble's unchanged aspect throws
>   O'er the fair Venus, but for ever fair;
> O'er the Laocoon's all eternal throes,
>   And ever-dying Gladiator's air,
> Their energy like life forms all their fame,
> Yet looks not life, for they are still the same.

. . . The line of Byron's thought seems to me to be taken straight from stanzas 2 and 3 of the "Grecian Urn" Ode, which was published nearly two years before the Fourth Canto of *Don Juan*.

No. 2 Leigh Hunt, *Lord Byron and Some of His Contemporaries* (London: Henry Colburn, 1828 2nd ed.), I, 434.

One passage is on a sculptured vase, representing a procession with music; upon which the author says, with an intensity of sentiment, at once original in the idea, and going home, like an old thought, to the heart—

[Quotes second stanza of "Ode on a Grecian Urn"]

Upon this beautiful passage, a sapient critic observed, that he should like to know how there could be music unheard.

No. 3 William Wordsworth. Markham L. Peacock, Jr., *The Critical Opinions of William Wordsworth* (Baltimore: Johns Hopkins, 1950), 290.

[Having expressed previously in "Praised to the Art" {sic. L.} almost the same thought as that of Keats's "Ode On a Grecian Urn," W.] felt a peculiar satisfaction. Not that he suggested any borrowing of the idea on the part of Keats.
Graves's Recollections, pp. 301-2. c. 1840.

> Praised be the Art whose subtle power could stay
> Yon cloud, and fix it in that glorious shape;
> Nor would permit the thin smoke to escape,
> Nor those bright sunbeams to forsake the day;
> Which stopped that band of travellers on their way,
> Ere they were lost within the shady wood;
> And showed the Bark upon the glassy flood
> For ever anchored in her sheltering bay.
> Soul-soothing Art! whom Morning, Noontide, Even,

Do serve with all their changeful pageantry;
Thou, with ambition modest yet sublime,
Here, for the sight of mortal man, hast given
To one brief moment caught from fleeting time
The appropriate calm of blest eternity.

No. 4 Emily Dickinson.

I died for beauty, but was scarce
Adjusted in the tomb,
When one who died for truth was lain
In an adjoining room.

He questioned softly why I failed?
'For beauty,' I replied.
'And I for truth—the two are one
We brethren are,' he said.

No. 5 Matthew Arnold, "John Keats." First published as preface to
a selection of Keats' poetry in Ward's *English Poets,* vol. iv, 1880.
Reprinted in *Essays in Criticism, Second Series,* 1888.

The truth is that 'the yearning passion for the Beautiful,' which
was with Keats, as he himself truly says, the master-passion, is
not a passion of the sensuous or sentimental man, is not a passion
of the sensuous or sentimental poet. It is an intellectual and
spiritual passion. . . .
For to see things in their beauty is to see things in their truth,
and Keats knew it. 'What the Imagination seizes as Beauty must
be Truth,' he says in prose; and in immortal verse he has said
the same thing—

'Beauty is truth, truth beauty,—that is all
Ye know on earth, and all ye need to know.'

No, it is not all; but it is true, deeply true, and we have deep
need to know it.

No. 6 Mrs. Oliphant, *The Literary History of England* (New York:
Macmillan, 1886), II, 279-280.

. . . his *Ode to a Nightingale,* that to *Autumn,* the loveliest embodiment of the "season of mists and mellow fruitfulness," that
On a Greek Vase [sic], which contains so wonderful a description
of the immortal life of the past, arrested in a moment of fullest
activity and preserved for ever by art: would still secure his immortality. These verses are above criticism, and cannot be read
but with a gentle rapture, that supreme satisfaction of ear and

mind which makes us linger and repeat and part unwillingly with
the liquid lines.

No. 7 Roden Noel, *Essays on Poetry and Poets* (London: Kegan
Paul, 1886), 151, 169.

He might, or might not have modified that profession of faith
which has become celebrated, that "Beauty is Truth, and Truth
Beauty." But he would hardly have thus expressed himself at all,
if he had not been uttering a deliberate intellectual conviction.
And the saying is capable of ample vindication. It is Platonic, if
only you take into your conception elements not in themselves
beautiful, but capable of being eventually harmonized with others
into a higher ideal of beauty than were at all realizable without
them. In fact, the full truth is concrete rather than abstract. It
must be that which corresponds to all our faculties, not to one or
two of them only. Hence, fuller vision is vision of the more rich,
full, concrete, and alive. . . . But that the sensuous element was
the most consummate in Keats can hardly be denied. . . .

The "Ode on a Grecian Urn" wonderfully enshrines the poet's
kinship with Greece, and with the spirit of her worship. There is
all the Greek measure and moderation about it also; a calm and
classic grace, with severe loveliness of outline. In form it is perfect.

No. 8 Sidney Colvin, *Keats* (London: Macmillan, 1887), 170-171.

The sight, or the imagination, of a piece of ancient sculpture
had set the poet's mind at work, on the one hand conjuring up
the scenes of ancient life and worship which lay behind and suggested the sculptured images; on the other, speculating on the
abstract relations of plastic art to life. The opening invocation is
followed by a string of questions which flash their own answer
upon us out of the darkness of antiquity—interrogatories which
are at the same time pictures—"What men or gods are these, what
maidens loth," etc. The second and third stanzas express with
perfect poetic felicity and insight the vital differences between
life, which pays for its unique prerogative of reality by satiety and
decay, and art, which in forfeiting reality gains in exchange permanence of beauty, and the power to charm by imagined experiences even richer than the real. Then the questioning begins
again, and yields the incomparable choice of pictures—

> "What little town by river or sea shore,
>   Or mountain built with peaceful citadel,
>   Is emptied of its folk, this quiet morn?"

In the answering lines—

> "And, little town, thy streets for evermore
> Will silent be; and not a soul to tell
> Why thou art desolate, can e'er return"—

in these lines there seems a dissonance, inasmuch as they speak of the arrest of life as though it were an infliction in the sphere of reality, and not merely, like the instance of such arrest given farther back, a necessary condition in the sphere of art, having in that sphere its own compensations. But it is a dissonance which the attentive reader can easily reconcile for himself; and none but an attentive reader will notice it. Finally, dropping the airy play of the mind backward and forward between the two spheres, the poet consigns the work of ancient skill to the future, to remain,

> "in midst of other woe
> Than ours, a friend to man, to whom thou say'st,
> Beauty is truth, truth beauty;"

thus proclaiming in the last words what, amidst the gropings of reason and the flux of things, is to the poet and artist—at least to one of Keats's temper—an immutable law.

No. 9 William Michael Rossetti, *Life of John Keats* (London: Walter Scott, 1887), 194-198.

As no poet had more capacity for enjoyment than Keats, so none exceeded him in the luxury of sorrow. Few also exceeded him in the sense of the one moment irretrievable; but this conception in its fulness belongs to the region of morals yet more than of sensation, and the spirit of Keats was almost an alien in the region of morals. . . . That axiom which concludes the "Ode on a Grecian Urn" . . . is perhaps the most important contribution to thought which the poetry of Keats contains: it pairs with and transcends

> "A thing of beauty is a joy forever."

. . . In the Ode, the axiom is put forward as the message of the sculptured Grecian Urn "to man," and is thus propounded as being of universal application. It amounts to saying—"Any beauty which is not truthful (if any such there be), and any truth which is not beautiful (if any such there be), are of no practical importance to mankind in their mundane condition: but in fact there are none such, for, to the human mind, beauty and truth are one and the same thing." To debate this question on abstract grounds is not in my province: all that I have to do is to point out that Keats's perception and thought crystallized into this axiom as the sum and substance of wisdom for man, and that he has bequeathed it to us to ponder in itself, and to lay to heart as the secret of his writings.

No. 10 Edmund Clarence Stedman, *The Nature and Elements of Poetry* (Boston: Houghton Mifflin, 1892), 67-68, 187-188.

A stanza from the "Ode on a Grecian Urn" describes, and rivals in verse, the ravishing power of a bit of sculpture to perpetuate arrested form and attitude—yes, even the suggestion of arrested music:—[quotes second stanza of Ode]

These undying lines not only define by words the power and limits of the sculptor, but are almost a matchless example of the farthest encroachment poetry can make upon sculpture's own province.

. . . .

If all natural things make for beauty, . . . then truth and beauty, in the last reduction are equivalent terms, and beauty is the unveiled shining countenance of truth. But a given truth, to be beautiful, must be complete. . . . Truth which is half a lie is intolerable. A certain kind of preachment, antipathetic to the spirit of poesy, has received the name of didacticism. Instinct tells us that it is a heresy in any form of art. Yet many persons, after being assured by Keats that the unity of beauty and truth is all we know or need to know, are perplexed to find sententious statements of undisputed facts so commonplace and odious. Note, meanwhile, that Keats' assertion illustrates itself by injuring the otherwise perfect poem which contains it. So obtrusive a moral lessens the effect of the "Ode on a Grecian Urn." In other words, the beauty of the poem would be truer without it.

No. 11 Archibald Lampman, "The Character and Poetry of Keats." Written in 1893, this essay was edited by E. K. Brown, and first published in the *University of Toronto Quarterly*, XV (July, 1946), 356-372. This excerpt is from pages 370-371.

It seems to me that the "Ode on a Grecian Urn" marks an epoch in English literature. It was a sort of revelation. It has added grace to thousands of refined minds, and lifted the whole plane of intellectual enjoyment. . . . It is interesting not only for the incomparable loveliness of the imagery and versification, but as an enunciation of the fruitful idea which up to this time Keats had had most at heart. It is his clearest expression of pure and

happy trust in Beauty—Beauty as comprehending all things that
the soul need care for. The effect upon the soul of a thing of perfect beauty is not so much that of completeness as of boundlessness
like eternity. Thought cannot go beyond it, and must rest in its
presence contented and absorbed. What can it be therefore but
Truth, or, as Keats thought, the only absolute Truth?

No. 12   Robert Bridges, "Critical Introduction," *Poems of John
Keats,* ed. G. Thorn Drury (London: Lawrence and Bullen, 1895),
lxvi.

Next, and disputing place with the last [of the odes, as poorest
in quality] comes the *Grecian Urn.* The thought as enounced in
the first stanza is the supremacy of ideal art over Nature, because
of its unchanging expression of perfection; and this is true and
beautiful; but its amplification in the poem is unprogressive,
monotonous, and scattered, the attention being called to fresh
details without result (see espec. 11. 21-24, anticipated in 15, 16),
which gives an effect of poverty in spite of the beauty. The last
stanza enters stumbling on a pun, but its concluding lines are
very fine, and make a sort of recovery with their forcible directness.

No. 13   William C. Wilkinson, "Two Odes of Keats's: I. On a
Grecian Urn," *Bookman, V* (New York, 1897), 217-219.

To interpret the urn and the artistic language inscribed on it,
as an expression of Greek delight in life and beauty, and to set
this charming ideal in subtly suggested pathetic contrast with the
reality which we all know in the world of human experience—the
imaginative ever-during perfection of that, over against the flawed
and fleeting character of this—such I take to be the true idea and
motive of the poem. The first two stanzas give us the key, set the
tone; which is charmingly left lingering in the ear in the last line
of the second stanza:

> For ever wilt thou love and she be fair.

. . . The finely restrained mere suggestion of the contrast between
what the poet sees on the urn and what is true in real life is here
a far better effect, both of beauty and of pathos, than the broader
statement at the close of the next stanza:

> All breathing human passion far above,
>   That leaves a heart high sorrowful and cloyed,
>   A burning forehead, and a parching tongue.

These lines, indeed, enforce . . . an emphasis which is excessive, which partly breaks the . . . [poem's] spell of cheerful, even joyous, imaginative interpretation—which, in short, impairs the harmony of tone in the ode. . . . If the poet had written instead something in the spirit of this:

> All chance of change from perfect far above
>   Never with sweet fruition to be cloyed,
>   Never with bitter disappointment stung,

he would have avoided the jar in tone, and have kept closer to his real theme. It must . . . be added that this whole stanza too nearly repeats the thought of the stanza preceding . . . [and] I never escape a feeling that the word "happy" is somewhat overworked. . . . [My revisions] are by no means submitted as replacements, but only as indications . . . of what the poet . . . should have done, in order to preserve harmony of tone in his poem. . . . Use and wont will naturally work in favour of the familiar original lines in each case; and any disturbance of what has been hitherto accepted will inevitably at first be unwelcome. . . . My point is that . . . Keats fixed for himself . . . a certain tone . . . which he ought to have maintained throughout . . . but which at certain points he violated, to the harm of his poem.

The first seven lines of the next stanza are exquisite in feeling, in fancy, and in phrase. . . . The frugal use of adjectives and the absolute felicity in choice of them . . . —how altogether admirable. . . . [But then we] come to the closing lines and encounter a recurrence of the discordant over-emphasis of unhappy suggestion:

> Ah! little town, thy streets for evermore
>   Will silent be; and not a soul to tell
>   Why thou art desolate, can e'er return.

This unexpected (not to say ungenuine) melancholy breaks once more the harmony of tone in the poem. The idea of "desolation" does not belong at all to the "emptying" on some "pious morn" of a "little town" for holiday and festival. The sad note, therefore, struck in the word "desolate" is here a false one. To have written:

> Thrice happy little town, for evermore
>   It shall with all thy pleasant streets be well,
>   Nor war nor waste can leave thy homes forlorn,

would sufficiently have suggested the heightening contrast underlying, and at the same time have left the harmony of cheerful tone undisturbed. . . .

But the chief artistic fault of this charming poem lies exactly at the point at which its chief excellence should be found, and that is the conclusion: [quotes last four lines]

What is the message intended by the poet from the urn to man? Simply that beauty is truth and that truth is beauty? The quotation-marks seems to answer yes. . . . If so, then we have the poet turning suddenly from his apostrophe to the urn . . . and addressing an audience of his fellow-men . . . —an abrupt change of direction for the poem, which is certainly not good art. . . . If, on the other hand, the quotation-marks ought to embrace the whole of the last two lines, and thus to incorporate what were otherwise the poet's comment into the text itself of the urn's message, then we have the urn delivering to man a weighty sentence, as of ultimate wisdom not before discerned by him, and accompanying that sentence with an implicit intimation that he already knew the lesson inculcated.

In either way the conclusion is infelicitous—this without reference . . . to the validity and value of the thought involved . . . [or] to the fitness of attributing such a message to the urn. But the idea of "truth" seems to me . . . foisted in with violence. . . . "Beauty," according to the spirit of the poem in its whole tenor from the beginning up to the present point, is the only idea naturally suggested. A paradox and a falsity like "Beauty is truth, truth beauty," and especially the absurdity added, that such a paradox is all that men need to know on earth, may . . . reveal the immature and excessive passion of the poet for mere beauty; but as a maxim to live by, or to write, to judge, or to enjoy poetry by, it is surely a delusion. . . . I should much more believingly have listened to the lovely urn telling us, for example, "Beauty is joy"; and then the poet might have commented so as to make the last two lines read:

> "Beauty is joy"—as were that wisdom all
> We needed, in so sad a world, to know!

Still better, perhaps, it might be to let the message have the whole of the rest of the poem, and . . . say:

> "Possessing beauty, thou possessest all;
> Rest at this goal, nor farther seek to go."

If one wished to get rid of the over-strong word "woe," and at the same time of the awkward discord of tenses involved in "shall remain" and "say'st," a change like this, affecting two more lines, might serve:

> Age after age, unchangeably serene,
>   Thou smilest sweet rebuke to our unrest,
> Preaching this wisdom with thy cheerful mien:
> "Possessing beauty thou possessest all;
>   Pause at that goal nor farther push thy quest."

Some closing, at any rate, that kept to the idea of "beauty" apart from the idea of "truth" would have been fitter to the character of the urn as described, would have been more in harmony with the general spirit of the ode, and would besides, have proposed a less indigestible paradox for the nurture of our minds.

No. 14   C. E. Pickard, "Keats Improved," *Critic* (New York, 1897), XXVII n. s., 388.

A witty and incisive rejoinder to the Wilkinson article.

No. 15   Arthur Symons, *The Romantic Movement in English Poetry* (London: Constable, 1909), 303, 306-7, 313-314.

But Keats, remember, was not the friend of beauty, he was her very human lover, sighing after her feverishly. With him beauty was always a part of feeling, always a thing to quicken his pulses, and send the blood to his forehead. . . . With Shelley beauty was an ideal thing, not to be touched by human hands. . . . It is characteristic that Shelley writes his confession of faith in a 'Hymn to Intellectual Beauty'; Keats, in an 'Ode on a Grecian Urn.' . . .

Keats, at a time when the phrase had not yet been invented, practised the theory of art for art's sake. . . . [His] is the temperament of the artist, to whom art is more than life, and who, if he realises that 'Beauty is Truth, Truth Beauty,' loves truth for being beautiful and not beauty for its innermost soul of spiritual truth. . . .

Keats' sense of form, if by form is meant perfection rather of outline than of detail, was by no means certain. Most poets work only in outline: Keats worked on every inch of his surface. Perhaps no poet has ever packed so much poetic detail into so small a space, or been so satified with having done so. Metrically, he is often slipshod; with all his genius for words, he often uses them incorrectly. . . . In the 'Ode on a Grecian Urn,' two lines near the end seem to halt by the way, are not firm and direct in movement:—

> 'Thou shalt remain, in midst of other woe
> Than ours, a friend to man, to whom thou say'st.'

That is slipshod writing, both as intellectual and as metrical structure; and it occurs in a poem which is one of the greatest lyrical poems in the language. . . . [But] however many faults we may find, we shall end, as we began, by realising that they do not matter.

No. 16 W. J. Courthope, *A History of English Poetry* (London: Macmillan, 1910), VI, 352-354.

It is, however, in his *Odes* that Keats has most enduringly enshrined his idea of "Abstract Beauty." In these—particularly the *Nightingale, Autumn,* and the *Grecian Urn*—the underlying feeling is always the same, a yearning desire to merge the imagination in some ideal form of life apart from experience and action. All Keats' personality seems to be breathed into these compositions. . . .

The epigram [which concludes the *Grecian Urn*] will not bear intellectual examination. A proposition of Euclid is true but it is not beautiful; nor, if it were, could the mere knowledge of what is ideally beautiful satisfy the wants of the soul; but as an example of the power of Poetry at once to illustrate and to supplement the functions of a sister Art, the Ode itself is a marvellous performance.

No. 17 David Watson Rannie, "Keats's Epithets," *Essays and Studies by Members of the English Association,* Vol. III (Oxford: Clarendon, 1912), 107-113.

In order to feel the force of Keats's epithets in his poetry we must not be content with considering them singly. Much of their power is in their mere abundance; and we shall never realize what Keats could do with adjectives until we hear or see them, so to say, in mass. Every reader knows how much the poet relies on plural effects of epithet—on repetition, multiplication, and accumulation: [quotes stanza 3, lines 21-26.]
When the whole stanza is carefully read, it is evident that the six-fold repetition of 'happy' is meant to express, by strong and subtle rhythmical emphasis, the wholesome purity of the emotion portrayed on the urn, in contrast with the inferior emotion of acted experience, the comparative unwholesomeness of which is, in turn, expressed by a little group of noteworthy epithets:

> All breathing human passion far above,
> And leaves a heart *high-sorrowful* and *cloyed,*
> A *burning* forehead and a *parching* tongue.

.   .   .   .

What light do Keats's epithets throw on the working of his imagination; i.e. on his efforts to express the beautiful or powerful truth of things in an interrelated world?

We may begin by making two negative generalizations.

1. Keats's epithets are collectively novel, striking, and indicative of the most careful verbal option and even invention; and yet we cannot describe them as making any strong appeal to the imagination. Their suggestiveness is limited. . . . They are the epithets of a great artist, but not of a fastidious . . . one.

2. They show constant regard for beauty of sound and archaic picturesqueness, yet . . . their chief interest lies in their meaning, in their success for characterization.

We come now to what is more positive.

3. Keats's epithets . . . are statical; i.e. they characterize objects in repose rather than movement. . . . Keats's subject-matter, expressed by his nouns, is concrete rather than abstract. His . . . themes are, not God, but this god or that god. . . . It follows naturally that Keats's epithets are material and sensuous rather than spiritual. . . .

So far as vision is concerned, they are epithets of tone rather than colour. . . .

It is to touch and taste that he makes his chief sensuous appeals. . . .

4. We are now ready to make our last reflection on Keats's epithets, namely, that they are distinctly the epithets of an artist of the type to which painters and sculptors belong. If, for the moment, we choose to divide poets into three classes, those who paint (or carve), those who sing, and those who prophesy, we must unhesitatingly place Keats in the first class.

No. 18 C. H. Herford, "Keats," *Cambridge History of English Literature,* Vol. XII (Cambridge, 1914), 99.

In the nearly contemporary *Ode on a Grecian Urn,* the symbolism of the urn-figures became far more vital [than it had been in *Indolence.*] From the drowsed intoxication of the senses, he rises to a glorious clear-eyed apprehension of the spiritual eternity which art, with its 'unheard melodies,' affords. The three consummate central stanzas have themselves the impassioned serenity of great sculpture. Only less noble are the daring and splendid imagery of the opening, and the immortal paradox of the close. . . . The worship of beauty is the clue to everything in Keats. . . .

[In the *Grecian Urn*,] he contemplates the passing of 'breathing human beauty' from the serene heights of eternal art. . . .

No. 19   Albert Mordell, *The Erotic Motive in Literature* (New York: Boni and Liveright, 1919), 199-205.

> In his introductory chapter, Mordell explains that "this work is an endeavor to apply some of the methods of psychoanalysis to literature. It attempts to read closely between the lines of an author's work. . . . A literary work is no longer regarded as a sort of objective product unrelated to its creator. . . . It is a personal expression and represents the whole man behind it. . . . Literature is a personal voice the source of which can be traced to the unconscious."

We know that [Keats'] sad love affair with Fanny Brawne, who coquetted with him, inspired a few poems directly addressed to her. . . . But it is rarely recognised that emotions connected with Fanny Brawne inspired his two most famous odes, the one to the Nightingale and the other to the Grecian Urn. . . . He loved beauty so much because of unrequited love. . . . Keats's love of beauty has a strong sexual component. His unfulfilled physical desires were sublimated into poems worshipping beauty. Art was his refuge. . . . The lines in the *Ode to a Grecian Urn* that particularly were written with Fanny in mind are those addressed to the lover of the Grecian Urn. . . .

Keats saw a resemblance between himself and that youth. He, too, was winning and near the goal, and he no more had her love than did the youth on the urn. He himself knew the passion

> "That leaves a heart high-sorrowful and cloy'd,
> A burning forehead and a parching tongue."

He had to accept his lot and pretend to see some advantage in it as he did in that of the youth on the urn:

> "More happy love! more happy, happy love!
> For ever warm and still to be enjoyed,
> For ever panting, and for ever young."

The poem is the song of unsatisfied desires. Keats, frustrated in his love, had one resource, to make poetry and create beauty out of his sorrow. To the future he too would be like that lover created by an ancient artist, panting for love ever young. The poem has such great appeal because it strikes a note in us all.

No. 20   A. C. Bradley, "Keats and 'Philosophy,' " orig. publ. in *The John Keats Memorial Volume,* 1921; repr. in *A Miscellany* (London: Macmillan, 1929), 189-192, 205-206.

The central article of the faith of Keats is given in the words "Beauty is truth, truth beauty." These two are reached, apprehended and expressed in different ways; beauty in or through sense and imagination, truth in or by "thought," "knowledge," or "philosophy." But the two are none the less one and the same; so that whatever is felt, perceived, imagined as beautiful, would, if adequately expressed in an intellectual form, be found a reality truly conceived; and truth, adequately transformed into the shape of "sensation" or imagination, would have turned into beauty. So, without aiming at precision in terminology, we may enlarge Keats's *dictum* "Beauty is truth, truth beauty."

In this faith he never wavered, but there is a difference in his attitude towards its two aspects. On the one hand, being a born poet, he desired truth, and the knowledge or philosophy that might lead to it, mainly, if not solely, for the enlargement or deepening that they might give to his perception and imagination of beauty; and, besides, he was *certain* that "what the Imagination seizes as Beauty must be truth," while he had not the same personal assurance (if we may so call it) that truth must be beautiful. On the other hand, while almost from the first he felt strongly his need of knowledge or philosophy, the feeling became more and more insistent as he advanced. . . .

What then did "philosophy" mean to him? Certainly not what it means when philosophy is contrasted with hasty passion, or when a man is advised to take his troubles philosophically. Not, on the other hand, philosophy in the strict or technical sense. With that he was, apparently, totally unacquainted; yet he always writes as though he had some philosophy of his own, though he hoped for much more. He speaks of the philosophy of Milton and Wordsworth, not of Locke or Berkeley. He uses the name of Plato for a rhyme in a jocular poem, but there is no sign that he had read a word of Plato or knew that Plato had written of beauty as well as truth. . . . The philosophy already known in his own experience and legible in his writings was evidently such reflection on human nature and life and the world as any thoughtful man may practise; a reflection intent, no doubt, but neither technical nor systematic. . . . In his poetry, it is hardly too much to say, death has become pure good, a friend, almost a Saviour. It delivers from "the weariness, the fever, and the fret." And so his favourite epithet for it is "quiet." . . . The death for which he longs, as he listens to the deathless Nightingale, is "easeful." The Grecian Urn, where the mortal beauty of life is no longer mortal, is the "bride of quietness." And yet here life, in putting on immortality, has lost nothing of its intensity; it has become "intenser." The "immortal bird" pours forth its soul abroad in ecstacy, and the love which no longer "leaves a heart high-sorrowful and cloy'd" is yet "for ever panting and for ever young." Would it be too bold to say that whenever the poet's soul in Keats touches and unites with the absolute and eternal beauty it is "in love with" death?

No. 21 Ernest de Sélincourt, *Oxford Lectures on Poetry* (Oxford: Clarendon, 1934 [Keats essay, 1921]), 196-197, 200, 206.

Love and death; from the clash of these two supreme experiences the genius of Keats reached its brief but splendid consummation.

Keats's relations with Fanny Brawne have been the subject of much comment, some of it from persons of impeccable breeding and of a sound physical constitution which precludes them from understanding the humiliating influence which a weakened body may exercise over the strongest mind. But no one could be severer upon Keats than he was upon himself. . . . He lacked the physical constitution to react healthily against the strain of his experience. How far under happier circumstances this love would have satisfied him is another matter. But the greatest poetry is not necessarily that of satisfied desire. . . . For his own bitter experience had awakened in him the longing to conceive a love

> All breathing human passion far above,
> That leaves a heart high-sorrowful and cloy'd,
> A burning forehead, and a parching tongue.

This tragic passion, though it wrought havoc with his body . . . opened up fresh vistas to his imagination and raised his art to heights that he had not yet scaled. . . . And what nature does in the eternal resurrection of her loveliness man can achieve by the creative energy of art. Such is the thought which inspires the *Ode to a Grecian Urn.* 'The form remains, the function never dies.' Art distils the beauty from a fleeting moment and gives it immortality. . . .

The *Odes* of Keats, like all great poetry, reveal to us no striking novelty of thought. The emotions that pulse through them are as old as man's aspirations and man's aching heart. . . . And this faith in the principle of beauty, held through all pain and disillusionment, brought to Keats its own reward. . . . The emotion that [his later poems] evoke is a spiritual triumph won from that very pain and passion which their beauty lays to rest. Are we wholly mistaken if, with Keats, we call that beauty, truth?

No. 22 Hugh I'Anson Fausset, *Keats: A Study in Development* (London: Martin Secker, 1922), 79-80, 83-84.

In his "Foreword" Fausset explains the principle upon which his book rests: "A close examination of Keats's poetry in the order of its composition, and of his letters in relation to his poetry, revealed to me a very logical and significant development from sensationalism to vision, from idealisation to idealism.

"This gradual definition of his genius, once grasped, should give new point to all he wrote."

The Odes on a Grecian Urn and to a Nightingale may be considered together. . . . In each the impermanence, the discord and the decay of man is contrasted with a state of existence which Keats visions as eternal and unalterable. In neither case is the permanence one of fact; the decoration of the urn is liable to decay or the accident of breakage: the song of the nightingale passes with the night, and the songster is certainly no more eternal than man is. . . . In both cases then, it is the idea of beauty, expressed through a work of art and a voice of nature, which he contrasts with the fact of man. . . . The "Attic shape" is within the dimensions of space in fact, it is beyond it in the idea which it embodies through fact. . . .

"Beauty is Truth," Keats summarised it, and it was not to the sensual ear that he spoke the word, and yet in the very arbitrary contrast between the mortality of man and the immortality of a perfect song, he was judging the one on a basis of sense, and the other as a spiritual symbol. Both odes represent with a difference a passionate escape from the hedging facts of life into the realm of pure sensation, which is immortal only as long as the identification of sense with the song or the work of art lasts, but which fades when the connection is severed. . . . It is of little matter that "Old age shall this generation waste" for "Beauty is truth" and shall survive the ages. Such a philosophy is indeed imperfect if it allow the eternal idea of beauty to a work of art and refuse it to man, of whose spirit every perfect work of art is the expression: but Keats has laid his hand, if tentatively, upon a principle, by which life as well as art comes to have a reason, and is not merely an accepted sensation. In wedding beauty with truth he consciously related sensuousness to idealism, and in hailing the permanence of art above that of nature, he affirmed, however tentatively, that it is the duty of human reason to induce order in the confusion of life by control and selection.

No. 23 Henry Van Dyke, *Companionable Books* (New York, Scribner's, 1922), 175-176.

He is in the highest and best sense of the word a juvenile poet—"mature," as Lowell says, but mature, as genius always is, within the boundaries and in the spirit of his own season of life. The very sadness of his lovely odes, "To a Nightingale," "On a Grecian Urn," "To Autumn," "To Psyche," is the pleasant melancholy of the springtime of the heart. . . . The poetry of Keats . . . endures, and will endure, in English literature, because it is the embodiment of *the spirit of immortal youth.*

No. 24   Sir Arthur Quiller-Couch, *Charles Dickens and Other Victorians* (New York: Putnam's, 1925), 159-160.

Turn now to Keats and you are returned upon *mere* poetry, in the Latin sense of *mere.* Keats has no politics, no philosophy of statecraft, little social feeling: he is a young apostle of poetry for poetry's sake.

> Beauty is truth, truth beauty,—that is all
> Ye know on earth; and all ye need to know.

But of course, to put it solidly, that is a vague observation—to anyone whom life has taught to face facts and define his terms, actually an *uneducated* conclusion, albeit most pardonable in one so young and ardent.

No. 25   Amy Lowell, *John Keats* (Boston: Houghton Mifflin, 1925), II, 242-243.

No poem of Keats's has had its origins more diligently sought for than the *Grecian Urn.* But in this case such searching seems peculiarly unnecesary. Keats had spent two years intermittently gazing at the Elgin marbles, he had pored again and again over volumes of drawings from the antique in Haydon's studio, he had read Goldsmith's *History of Greece* at Haydon's instigation, and he had done all this with an attention and imagination ever on the alert. How keen was his interest in these things may be seen by the fact that a tracing from a plate of the so-called Sosibos vase, made by him, was discovered in the Dilke Collection. . . . With various of Claude Lorraine's pseudo-classic pictures, he was also familiar. . . . Granted all these things, they are the merest spark of a match to flash the eager fire of his imagination. In no other poem that Keats wrote do we see his imagination more actively at work, or more perfectly master of its own expression. The poem is well-nigh flawless from beginning to end. It is a picture, an experience, and a creed, all in one. It is the world without and the world within. . . . Where else does his imagination give us a picture with such economy of detail as in his lines about the little town? What a lightning stroke of genius to depict it only to empty it, leaving it solitary in the morning sun, and, by a swift transition from gay to grave, evoking its eternal desolation. . . . The poem is a magnificent example of joy through resignation, for Keats had looked with ecstasy and anguish at life, at love, at art, and had learnt to submit to immutable law. . . .

I think that when Keats wrote the *Grecian Urn* he was at the very zenith of his development, more entirely single, whole, and undivided, more completely master of his qualities, all of them, than ever before or ever again.

No. 26 Clarence Dewitt Thorpe, *The Mind of John Keats* (New York: Oxford, 1926), v, 127-128, 134-135, 148.

My first objective was to discover an adequate interpretation for the famous lines from the *Ode on a Grecian Urn* which identify truth and beauty. . . . [I]t seems to me these lines have never been, up to this time, satisfactorily explained. And one reason is, I feel convinced, that they have never been regarded in the light of Keats's complete aesthetic theory. In my own interpretation of them, I have found it necessary to take into account all of the poet's ideas of his art, to which these lines are both the key and culmination. . . . Beauty, with Keats, was not only the open sesame to poetic life and truth, it was truth itself: "What the Imagination seizes as Beauty must be Truth, whether it existed before or not." . . . [T]he method of the imagination as opposed to reasoning and the scientific approach is that of emotionalized intuitive perception. A sense of spiritual reality which the mind apprehends imaginatively, then, or immediately rather than indirectly, is Beauty; this is also Truth. . . .

With reference to a work of art, Beauty is the emotional recognition of the life-truth revealed there. . . . Let us look for a moment at what Keats sees in the various pieces of art that formed the inspiration for the [*Ode on a Grecian Urn.*] What he really does in the ode is to describe a series of pictures or scenes that he imagines must have formed the basis for the artist's work, and to give us his own speculations growing out of his contemplation of the sculptured representation of these scenes. The external aspects of the urn do not constitute its beauty. It is rather that the symbols executed here, themselves a product of mind and soul, still contain within themselves a dynamic something that has power to kindle the imagination of a sympathetic observer, who not only is able to re-create the particular bit of life that furnished the material through which the artist worked, but can also catch the gleam beyond, the vision of the universal that the creator of the piece himself conceived. That is what Keats saw in the urn, and in this is its beauty.

. . . This comes to the mind of Keats in a pleasurable wave of recognition. It is pleasurable because he detects, starting out at him from the fair chiselled form, waves of intuitive whisperings that seize his imagination and set it aflame; it is pleasurable, moreover, because in the intensity of speculation that follows, there comes a sense of discovery of truth; and it is not mere fact or logical conclusion he perceives, nor is it a moral precept, nor a religious idea; it is rather like a revelation of a principle of existence, a perception of a law of life, an insight into the universal human heart. So to Keats truth arrived at through emotionalized imaginative perception is beauty, and beauty is truth. . . .

In the *Ode on a Grecian Urn* art in its enduring permanence is compared with brief and fleeting human life, and there is quite as clear an implication as to the eternity of the Truth and Beauty which the artist has captured and fixed in his medium of relatively temporary art form. . . . Grecian urns of whatever beauty shall crumble away, but the human passions, the universal truths represented there, shall endure.

No. 27   H. W. Garrod, *Keats* (Oxford: Clarendon, 1926 [1950]), 72, 101-104.

Note to the Second Edition: My general view of the character of Keats' poetry remains somewhat different from that which is still fashionable. I still 'think him the great poet he is only when the senses capture him, when he finds truth in beauty, that is to say, when he does not trouble to find truth at all.'

Let me say, then, quite simply, that I think the Odes of Keats worth *study*, worth, that is, some pains of scholarship. . . . [I]t is yet true that study is the parent of appreciation. If the Odes of Keats are as perfect as I think them, and as they are accounted, they deserve to call forth in us some better element than our faculty for gush. . . . The *Grecian Urn* we may suppose to have been written in a mood of revulsion from the thesis of *Melancholy* . . . [which is] the world of the poet, though he perish in it. The *Grecian Urn* presents, in fact, the same world, the world of beauty and human passions, only fixed by art. The lover whom the Urn figures loves, not a 'beauty that must die,' but that which, from the nature of art, 'cannot fade.' . . .

The first four stanzas of the Ode achieve a faultless harmonization of thought, sentiment, and language. But I have never been able to think the last stanza worthy of the rest, or consistent with it. I dislike . . . the assonance *Attic . . . attitude,* in the first line of it, and the obscurely intended affectation 'brede.' I dislike, in the fifth line, the metrical carry-over 'As doth eternity'—this is the only place in the Ode where a clear separation is not maintained between quatrain and sestet. . . . Indeed, the movement of the whole of the sestet is 'choppy.' But more serious . . . —and a fault of which these are symptomatic—the connexions of the stanzas both internally and in respect of the stanzas preceding are difficult. The theme of what has gone before is the arrest of beauty, the fixity given by art to forms which in life are fluid and impermanent, and the appeal of art from the senses to the spirit. The theme of the final stanza is the relation of beauty to truth, to thought. Nothing has prepared the transition to this. The first half of the stanza, moreover, makes it the effect of art, of this *'cold* pastoral' . . . that it 'teases us out of thought, as doth Eternity.' Yet the effect upon which our attention has hitherto been concentrated is that the Urn lifts us out of sense into thought. . . . What has happened? The beholder, I suppose, kept so long from sense in the region of thought, is now assailed by misgivings about the reality of a work of art thus remote from the warm breathing life of the sensible world. The figures of the Urn become for him, suddenly, a *'cold* Pastoral'—cold with the character of everything that is enduring. . . . The second half of the stanza . . . seeks to allay the doubt set up; to allay it by the thesis that there is nothing real but the beautiful, and nothing beautiful but the real.

I find these difficulties, then, in the final stanza. . . . But every reader, I think, in some degree feels them, feels a certain uneasiness. The lines *are* difficult; they do not, either in thought or feeling, hang with the rest of the Ode. More than that I would not urge. . . . Perhaps the fourth stanza is more beautiful than any of the others—and more true. The trouble is that it is a little too true. Truth to his main theme has taken Keats rather farther than he meant to go. The pure and ideal art of the 'cold Pastoral,' this 'silent form,' *has* a cold silentness which in some degree saddens him. In the last lines of the fourth stanza, especially the last three lines, . . . every reader is conscious, I should suppose, of an undertone of sadness, of disappointment. This pure and cold art makes, in fact, a less appeal to Keats than the Ode as a whole would pretend; and when, in the lines which follow these lines, he indulges the jarring apostrophe 'Cold Pastoral,' . . . he has said more than he meant—or than he wished to mean.

No. 28   Raymond D. Havens, "Concerning the 'Ode on a Grecian Urn,' " *Modern Philology*, XXIV (1926-7), 209-214.

No. 29   B. Ifor Evans, "Keats and the Golden Ass," *Nineteenth Century*, C (August 1926), 263, 269-270.

> Possibly the most satisfactory element in this product of poetic maturity is the group of *Odes;* here his imagination is magical and yet disciplined by a certain rigidity of form which adds to the enchantment. Certain of these *Odes* have been sufficiently praised. Indeed, the *Grecian Urn* poem, with its concluding passage on 'Truth is Beauty,' has called forth unnecessary quantities of critical ink. Keats explained all that he meant by that phrase in a journal letter to his brother and sister-in-law:
>
>> I am certain of nothing but the holiness of the Heart's affections, and the truth of Imagination. What the Imagination seizes as Beauty must be truth—whether it existed before or not.
>
> If that does not explain Keats's mind, no superstructure of critical elucidation will ever do so. . . .
>
> In the *Ode on a Grecian Urn* Keats elaborates more fully than anywhere else the suggestion which he first saw for himself in the *Psyche* poem. The figures on the urn are symbols of action which stimulate the mind to imaginative experience. If instead of those shapes we had the living counterparts of which they are the image, the music would pass, the loves die, the joy be made bitter by regret; but on the urn they are 'unravish'd,' perpetual figures on that mental shrine of Psyche, by which the perdurability of the affections arising from the imagination is maintained. . . . Sensuousness and the aftermath of senation on the one hand, and the retention of Beauty as first perceived on the other, those seem to be the ideas which fascinate him. . . .

No. 30   E. V. Weller, ed., *Keats and Mary Tighe: The Poems of Mary Tighe with Parallel Passages from the Work of John Keats* (New York, MLA, 1928).

> Weller claims Mary Tighe was a very powerful influence on all Keats' poems, especially, among others, on "Ode on a Grecian Urn." In his book, an extreme example of source-hunting, he indexes all the relevant passages, some of which seem farfetched.

No. 31   W. P. Ker, *Form and Style in Poetry* (London: Macmillan, 1928), 120-121.

The thought in the *Grecian Urn* . . . is still the theme of the life of poetry, the method is still poetical and imaginative, without the touch of abstract and purely philosophical speculation which may be found in Shelley. This is what makes the *Grecian Urn* so difficult to understand. There is no alloy of prose thinking. . . . The thought in the *Grecian Urn* is so thoroughly poetical that it may be mistaken by a careless reader for a fanciful conceit. . . . The work of his fancy about the Urn is not a transformation of sober reality into a pleasantly lively vision—it is a raid into the eternal world. . . . The poem itself effects what the poem speaks about. . . . It is the poem of Keats that remains, to do what he describes the Grecian Urn as doing.

No. 32 Royall Snow, "Heresy Concerning Keats," *PMLA*, XLIII (1928), 1142-1149.

One may very reasonably ask whether Keats ever even said "Beauty is truth," and the answer is: No, he probably did *not* say it, nor anything like it.

The confusion which arises when we accept the guileless statement as his may be summarized briefly. For four strophes the whole emotional value of the *Ode on a Grecian Urn* has been based upon the poignant transiency of human beauty and passion. Suddenly there comes the fifth and concluding strophe which declares that this "silent form," the urn, "dost tease us out of thought," after which it immediately advances a theory of aesthetics—and aesthetic theory is usually considered to have some connection with conscious cerebration. Moreover, the theory advanced implies that the *fact* of beauty is sufficient . . . in other words that its *transiency* is no matter, and that in four-fifths of the poem we have responded to an emotional appeal which has no real validity.

That is nonsense and instinctively we feel it. The poem is so well loved precisely because that appeal *is* valid and universal. Though we crave a solution of the questions transiency raises in our minds, we scarcely crave *this* solution once its implications become clear—it is so completely false to John Keats. For this is the solution of the art-for-art's sake people, and no one can imagine him in such company. . . .

May it not be possible that . . . Keats never either meant nor made such a statement as "Beauty is truth"? We take the passage out of the context, find its meaning lucid, and then put it back into the text only to find this lucid meaning troublesome. Perhaps it would be safer to find the meaning while the passage was still in its context. . . .

Particularly, once the lines are restored to the poem, one must scrutinize that word "Beauty." What beauty? Out of the context "Beauty" is Abstract Beauty, or something else inhuman which approximates it, and parades in the fine dress of Initial Capitals. In the context Keats clearly has a *specific* beauty in mind and that specific beauty may be either one of two. First it may be the Urn, *qua* urn: something marble and, above all, permanent. That agrees perfectly "in principle," as the diplomats say when there is mischief afoot, with Abstract Beauty. But the talk of Abstract Beauty is of our making and Keats is, or may be, innocent. . . .

Or, secondly, the beauty that he has definitely in mind may be that of the figures on the urn. It is the urn which gives us a message ("Thou sayst" are Keats's words). To be grotesquely literal for a moment—does the urn contract its marble lips and labialize the statement "Beauty is truth"? Hardly. Or do the scenes upon the urn convey a certain idea? They do. And it is these scenes, not the urn *qua* permanent marble, which make the point on which Keats ends. This is so obvious as scarcely to deserve mention, and yet the equally obvious consequences seem not to have been noticed. The word "urn" is never once mentioned in the text, its shape, its proportion are unknown; even its material, marble, is unmentioned until the fifth strophe, when we learn that the *figures* on it are marble. It is the beauty of these figures which is "all Ye know on earth, and all ye need to know," and the beauty of these figures is the beauty of pipes and timbrels and wild ecstasy.

Read in its context, Keats is abandoning the problem as insoluble, not advancing a theory of aesthetic. If these scenes—and Keats—say anything, they say: Beauty is not truth, at least not in any permanent and abiding sense. Such reason, such truth as you will find in life is to be found in momentary ecstasy, and here only. This is not a novel doctrine. Keats has been both praised and blamed for leanings toward it elsewhere: he seems never to have been accused of advancing it here where he did advance it in a flat statment. . . .

In the fourth strophe, Keats returns from the question to the sensuous object with which he began. It is a pause, a beautiful pause, and yet a sorrowful one, concluding with a dying cadence and the deep melancholy of streets forever deserted. The instinct which led to that pause (quite aside from the gracious charm of the picture) was the instinct of genius. After the sharp reversals of the preceding stanzas we are left tranquil a moment; the original beauty with which we began is reaffirmed, but with its accumulated sadness. And then, frankly and swiftly, Keats turns to give such solution as he is able. "O Attic shape," he says,

> Thou, silent form, dost tease us out of thought
> As doth eternity

Which means exactly what it says—that thought (which we have built up *about* the urn in the strophes following the initial ecstasy) breaks down and vanishes if we abandon ourselves to the message of the urn. Ecstasy can submerge us as completely as eternity. But the message, ecstasy, the clue, is withheld so that his last word may literally be his last word.

> When old age shall this generation waste
> Thou shalt remain in midst of other woe
> Than ours, a friend to man.

A fixed shape shall remain with this as yet undisclosed solution, which is the best Keats can offer. So far this interpretation is orthodox enough:—but is the message of the urn that of the poetasters and the art-for-art's-sake people? Was the ardent Keats content to call a marble woman the highest aspiration of mankind? Or did he mean in that parenthetical "a friend to man" that the urn was triumphantly pagan and unaware that this Anglo-Saxon question even had existence? The urn spoke, but not with literal marble lips—its pictures spoke and of these the initial one, which struck Keats most forcibly, is that of maidens loth and mad pursuit, of pipes and timbrels and wild ecstasy. *This* is all we can and need to know.

So conceived, the *Ode on a Grecian Urn* has that essential emotional coherence which is of more consequence to a work of art than the intellectual validity of its ideas. . . . The conclusion of the *Grecian Urn* was an out-and-out and passionate declaration for the senses, curiously mingled with a tinge of desperation.

No. 33 Mary Shipman, "Orthodoxy Concerning Keats," *PMLA*, XLIV (1929), 929-934.

Miss Shipman undertakes to answer, point by point, the essay by Royall Snow above, displaying equal vigor if less humor.

No. 34 I. A. Richards, *Practical Criticism: A Study of Literary Judgment* (New York: Harcourt, Brace, 1929 [1946]), 183, 186-187.

The possibilities of human misunderstanding make up indeed a formidable subject for study, but something more can be done to elucidate it than has yet been attempted. Whatever else we may do by the light of nature, it would be folly to maintain that we should read by it. . . .

But Feeling (and sometimes Tone) may take charge of and operate through Sense in another fashion, one more constantly relevant in poetry. . . .

When this happens, the statements which appear in the poetry are there for the sake of their effects upon feelings, not for their own sake. Hence to challenge their truth or to question whether they deserve serious attention *as statements claiming truth,* is to mistake their function. The point is that many, if not most, of the statements in poetry are there *as a means* to the manipulation and expression of feelings and attitudes, not as contributions to any body of doctrine of any type whatever. . . . [W]ith 'philosophical' or meditative poetry there is great danger of a confusion which may have two sets of consequences.

On the one hand there are very many people who, if they read any poetry at all, try to take all its statements seriously—and find them silly. . . . On the other hand there are those who succeed too well, who swallow 'Beauty is Truth, truth beauty. . . .', as the quintessence of an aesthetic philosophy, not as the expression of a certain blend of feelings, and proceed into a complete stalemate of muddle-mindedness as a result of their linguistic naïvety.

No. 35   T. S. Eliot, "Dante," (1929), repr. *Selected Essays: 1917-1932* (New York: Harcourt, Brace, 1932), 230-231.

And I confess to considerable difficulty in analysing my own feelings, a difficulty which makes me hesitate to accept Mr. Richard's theory of "pseudo-statements." On reading the line which he uses,

> Beauty is truth, truth beauty . . .

I am at first inclined to agree with him, because this statement of equivalence means nothing to me. But on re-reading the whole Ode, this line strikes me as a serious blemish on a beautiful poem, and the reason must be either that I fail to understand it, or that it is a statement which is untrue. And I suppose that Keats meant something by it, however remote his truth and his beauty may have been from these words in ordinary use. And I am sure that he would have repudiated any explanation of the line which called it a pseudo-statement. . . . The statement of Keats seems to me meaningless: or perhaps the fact that it is grammatically meaningless conceals another meaning from me.

No. 36 Takeshi Saito, *Keats' View of Poetry* (London: Cobden-Sanderson, 1929).

> Pp. 40-43 are particularly relevant, as Saito argues that the last lines of the ode state "the all-in-all that artists know, and the most important thing of all that they should know." See below, C. M. Bowra, No. 69.

No. 37 John Middleton Murry, *Studies in Keats New and Old* (London: Oxford, 1930 [1939]), 71-91.

> One of the most devoted of all Keats scholars, Murry has published five books on Keats during the past three decades. The essay "Beauty is Truth . . . ," from which the excerpts below are taken, has remained substantially unchanged in the books on Keats published since 1930. In his first book on Keats, *Keats and Shakespeare* (1925), Murry had this to say of his method and purpose: "Above all, this book is not the exposition of a theory. In criticism I have but one theory, namely, to be loyal to the reality of the man whose works move me profoundly. . . . To know a work of literature is to know the soul of the man who created it, and who created it in order that his soul should be known. Knowledge of a work of literature which stops short of that . . . is not the real knowledge."

Diversity of opinion could hardly be more extreme than in these judgements. For Dr. Bridges [see No. 12] the final lines redeemed a poor poem; for Mr. Eliot [see No. 35] they spoil a good one; for Sir Arthur Quiller-Couch [see No. 24] they are ignorant and uneducated; for Mr. Richards [see No. 40] that still ambiguous entity which he calls a pseudo-statement. . . .

My own opinion concerning the value of those two lines *in the context of the poem itself* is not very different from Mr. Eliot's. . . . To my sense the lines disturb the subtle harmony of the poem. . . .

The direct and enigmatic proposition disturbs the poem, because it does not belong to the same kind of utterance. The poem, as a whole, advances on strong and subtle waves of the pure sensuous imagination. It ends dissonantly with a stark enunciation which, to that part of the human mind which is aroused by stark enunciation, must be a baffling paradox. . . .

We suspect that Dr. Bridges believes that . . . the poem really consists in the enunciation of the 'true and beautiful' thought that Art is supreme over Nature; and that this thought and the assertion that 'Beauty is Truth, Truth Beauty' are the same. If our suspicion is founded, it can be easily understood why the development of the thought in the poem seems to him 'unprogressive and monotonous,' and why the last stanza seems to him to make a 'sort of recovery by its forcible directness.' What has happened is that Dr. Bridges has misinterpreted the last stanza as an assertion of the supremacy of Art over Nature, he has then read this misinterpretation by main force into the first stanza, and has finally judged the poem by its inevitable failure to develop a thought which is not contained in the poem at all.

That Truth and Beauty of the kind which are manifest in the thought of the supremacy of Art over Nature are not the Truth and Beauty whose identity is asserted in the last stanza is obvious from one simple consideration. The vase whispers, and will whisper, to minds aching with the thought of human misery, 'Beauty is Truth, Truth Beauty'; and to the poet this whisper brings the comfort of a great finality. When he hears the words, he cries:

that is all
Ye know on earth, and all ye need to know.

That is, of course, in the literal and grammatical sense, untrue. It is not 'all we know'; and some of us do not know it at all. But Keats' meaning is unmistakable. If we know that 'Beauty is Truth, Truth Beauty,' we have attained the topmost stretch of human knowledge; we know, as it were, the secret—the one thing needful.

I do not believe that anybody could, and I am quite certain that Keats could not, have found this finality in the mere thought that Art is supreme over Nature, because of its unchanging expression of perfection. Had this been the thought which the Grecian Urn awakened in his mind, Keats would never have written his poem. . . .

What is it, then, that Keats was saying. We must pick up the clues to his meaning as we can. But one thing is certain. The message of the Grecian Urn is a message of comfort on human woe. . . . The time at which he wrote the *Ode on a Grecian Urn* was a time of grinding misery. Everything was being taken from him, a brother dead, a brother exiled, . . . his new-born love strangled at birth, his money gone, his life in question. Such was Keats' share of the human woe to which, he declared, the Grecian Urn brought comfort. It was more than a fair share of the misery of the world. . . .

What meaning, we have to ask, could the words 'Beauty is Truth, Truth Beauty' bear to a man who was suffering as Keats was suffering then, which could bring to him finality and peace? We do not have to ask, coldly, what is the meaning of 'Beauty is Truth'? . . . If we know anything of human life we know that words which contain a message of peace in moments such as Keats was then enduring will not be easy words. They may be simple, but they will not be easy. And as human beings we know more than this; we know that they must contain a great renunciation. Such a message is in the words: 'Not my will, but Thine be done' . . .

The Urn is . . . capable of making 'all disagreeables evaporate from their being in close relationship to Beauty and Truth.' The thought came to Keats as he was meditating on the effect of a painting; it was exemplified, he said, throughout *King Lear*—a dramatic poem. And the Grecian Urn . . . is something between a painting and a dramatic poem. It is a sculptured drama. And this is as important to remember as it is readily forgotten. The Grecian Urn of Keats' poem is not some hypothetical actual vase, but the Urn of his imagination. . . .

It is on this arrested action that Keats' imagination intensely plays. He envies the felicity of the participants who are immune from mortality and decay. But they are human still. Mortality and decay have slipped from them, like a garment; but that is all. They are mortals as we are; who have wandered unawares into an enchanted land, whence they can never return. Their felicity has its tinge of sorrow; the poet who began by envying, ends almost by pitying. They are, as it were, lost to humanity.

> And, little town, thy streets for evermore
> Will silent be; and not a soul to tell
> Why thou art desolate, can e'er return.

The happening is utterly human. It is to misconceive the poem completely to conceive it as a theorizing on some exquisite piece of decorative art. It is a drama of the pure imagination. A destiny falls upon some human beings; they pass into the spellbound land of eternity,

> All breathing human passion far above

and the poet who watches them, who indeed himself has cast the spell of eternal immobility upon them, envies and grieves for them. The Urn is the record of the lovely and yet fatal enchantment.

More exactly, the Grecian Urn is the symbol of a possibility of vision. . . . That is why the 'silent form doth tease us out of thought as doth eternity.' It is not that it is incomprehensible as is the abstract concept of eternity; but that it is terribly simple and lucid as is the eternal aspect of things of which it is a symbol. . . . What words can there be to describe this seeing of the world and of ourselves with a vision from which all passion has been dissolved away; with a vision which is unclouded by any desire or any regret; by any belief or any anxiety: this moment of untroubled lucidity in which we are unmoved spectators of the great drama of human destiny?

For this vision there are indeed no words. Keats declared it in the form: 'Beauty is Truth, Truth Beauty.' The words to many are meaningless. And it is certain that by no poring over the words themselves can the vision which they express be attained. Nor, probably, if we turn them about, like a jewel of many facets, will they reflect a gleam.

We may turn them in many ways. We may say that the Real is Beautiful. The answer straightway is that the Real is full of ugliness and pain. And this is true: who will deny it? But the Beauty of the Real is a Beauty which resides as surely in pain and ugliness as in beauty itself. There is the sorrow which makes

> Sorrow more beautiful than Beauty's self.

But that sorrow may still be called, by our human standards, beautiful. The Beauty of the Real is beyond this. It lies in the perfection of uniqueness which belongs to every thing, or thought, simply because it *is*.

But this is not Beauty. And indeed it is not what men commonly call Beauty. . . . None the less, the great sayings that 'God is Love,' and that 'Omnis existentia est perfectio,' have their meaning for those who understand them. Keats uttered another saying worthy to stand with these simple and lucid finalities. 'Beauty is Truth, Truth Beauty' belongs to the same order as they; nor can any one truly understand any one of these sayings without understanding the others.

For the only name for the faculty by which we can discern that element of Beauty which is present in every Fact, which we must discern in every Fact before it becomes Truth for us, is Love. Whether it is Love which discovers the Beauty in Fact, whereby it becomes Truth; or whether it is the Beauty of Fact which causes the motion of Love to arise in our souls, and so to discern its Truth—to such questions there is no answer, nor any need to answer them. The relation between these things is simple and inextricable. When we love a Fact, it becomes Truth; when we attain that detachment from our passions whereby it becomes possible for us to love all Facts, then we have reached our Peace. . . .

Whether or not it is easily intelligible, there is a meaning in

'Beauty is Truth, Truth Beauty' which satisfies the conditions which we proposed as necessary. It is simple, but not easy; and it involves a great renunciation. That the first condition is satisfied is abundantly evident from our efforts to expound it. It is its utter simplicity which makes it so impossible to explain. . . .

And perhaps it is equally evident that it involves a great renunciation. To attain the vision which Keats describes as the knowledge that 'Beauty is Truth, Truth Beauty' we are required to put away all our human desires and beliefs and anxieties. We have to forget all those cares, delightful or painful, which appertain to our animal existence. Our joys and sorrows must become remote as though they happened to others than ourselves, or to ourselves in some other mode of existence from which we have awakened as from a dream. . . . Than this no greater renunciation is possible.

To be detached from ourselves—that is the positive and ethical implication of 'Beauty is Truth, Truth Beauty,' and the act of entire self-renunciation which is necessarily involved in achieving that self-detachment is the justification of Keats' assertion that

> That is all
> Ye know on earth, and all ye need to know.

No. 38   John Hawley Roberts, "Poetry of Sensation or of Thought?" *PMLA,* XLV (1930), 1129-1139.

Roberts attempts to present a synthesis for the thesis and antithesis of the Snow-Shipman exchange (see above Nos. 32 and 33.) His belief is that in an early poem, "Sleep and Poetry," q.v., Keats had pointed out two opposed kinds of poetry, sensuous and philosophical; that his natural tendency was toward the first; but that he felt obliged to try to write the second. Succeeding poems, "Endymion" and "Hyperion" especially, show that Keats was unable, in spite of persistent efforts, to resolve this deeply-felt conflict. With regard to the Grecian Urn, he finds for Mr. Snow.

No. 39   Hoxie Neale Fairchild, *The Romantic Quest* (Philadelphia: Alfred Saifer, 1931), 403-406, 411-413, 421.

A test which is useful in applying [a realistic] attitude to critical works is to imagine the poet as reading the critic's interpretation of him, and to ask, not if the poet would like the critical portrait, but if he would recognize it as a portrait at all. Imagine, for example, Keats and Shakespeare reading John Middleton Murry's *Keats and Shakespeare.* Or imagine Keats alone reading Clarence Dewitt Thorpe's *The Mind of John Keats,* and learning that when he spoke of beauty he had meant "a subjective conception of truth reached through imaginative perception." When the same test is applied to H. W. Garrod's *Keats*, the results are less startling. The poet would at least feel that the book was about him, and not about Garrod's beautiful soul. Garrod is somewhat meagre and juiceless . . . but he does not write as if Keats were Dostoevsky. . . . Now the poems of Keats proclaim in every line that he was primarily a lover and a creator of sensuous beauty. That is the foreground fact with which all interpretation of Keats as a poet must begin. . . .

The conclusion of *Ode on a Grecian Urn* has been so grossly gushed over that "Beauty is truth, truth beauty" has become one of the most nauseating phrases in literature. This passage from the letter to Bailey will help to explain its meaning:

> I am certain of nothing but the holiness of the Heart's affections, and the truth of the imagination. What the Imagination seizes as Beauty must be Truth—whether it existed before or not,—for I have the same idea of all our passions as of Love: they are all, in their sublime, creative of essential Beauty.

The imagination seizes not only upon lovely objects but upon lovely human passions and distills from them the pure essence of the beautiful. If the truth is something solid and satisfying by which man can live, then beauty is the only truth that Keats knows.

Man has no clear conception of the truth which he is seeking, and he never finds it. But he believes that if he ever did find it, it would prove to be completely self-sufficient and final—a pure good in itself. In seeking truth, then, man seeks something that possesses non-instrumental finality. In actual life, however, almost everything is an instrument for doing or getting some other thing. There is always a step above this one, and the end is nowhere in sight. Yet there are certain steps on which we can pause and breathe so happily that we seem for a moment to have reached the top. There are elements of life which can be regarded as good in themselves: play (not professionalized football, but play); love (not propagating the species, but love); science (not applied mechanics, but science); philosophy (not the precepts of Polonius, but philosophy); religion (not teaching poor little boys to play basketball, but religion); and the fine arts (not saying pretty and wholesome things, but the fine arts). At their core these are ends, not means. They may be enjoyed for their own sake, and in this they are like that final truth of which we dream. For Keats, the one great self-sufficient activity is art. When he says "Beauty is truth, truth beauty," he means that esthetic experience shows us what the contemplation of truth would be like if we ever found it. He wisely makes the qualification, "That is all ye know on *earth*"; and then adds, in a thoroughly pragmatic spirit, "and all ye need to know"—meaning that this sense of a correspondence between the esthetic experience and the perception of truth will serve for the working purposes of human beings this side the grave. Although discordant influences sometimes draw Keats away from this position, it represents the only philosophy that he can be said to possess. We may call it estheticism if we remember that it is free from the decadence of Pater's disciples. Keats's veins are filled with blood, not with Pre-Raphaelite ink. . . . But it is sad to think of art as infinitely precious because nothing else is worth anything, and sad to think of that bold lover stretching out his arms through the centuries as happier than he who risks the penalty of a human kiss.

No. 40 I. A. Richards, *Mencius on the Mind* (London: Kegan Paul, 1932), 117.

In the pages immediately preceding this discussion, Richards cites examples of multiple definition of key concepts, including Truth and Beauty.

The reader will notice that a superfluity of meanings, not any lack of meaning, is the difficulty. The fact that the ranges of Beauty and Truth overlap at three points (B5 = T 2b; B 8 = T 5; B9 = T 4b) gives to the equivalence, either as a gesture or as having some indefensible sense, a peculiarly strong suasive force. And this accounts for its power *in the poem* (when, of course, it is not apprehended analytically) to convey that feeling of deep acceptance which is often a chief phase in the aesthetic experience. The poem is perhaps unusual in having an aesthetic experience for *subject* as well as for aim.

No. 41 Oscar Firkins, *The Bride of Quietness, and Other Plays* (University of Minnesota, 1932), 1-60.

An attempt to interpret the Ode through a play in five scenes, starting in ancient Greece at the moment of the making of the urn and ending on the day of Keats' death.

No. 42 Solomon F. Gingerich, "The Conception of Beauty in the Works of Shelley, Keats, and Poe," *Essays and Studies in English and Comparative Literature* (Ann Arbor: University of Michigan Press, 1932), 178-179.

His famous saying, "O for a life of Sensations rather than Thoughts!" is true only as applied to his earliest literary years, for he soon began to rationalize his love of the beautiful. The first step in this rationalization lay in his discovery of a principle of permanency in beauty. Sensations were always a joy—sensations and sense-imagery are basic in poetry, and their importance must not be minimized—but the discovery that there is something lasting in beauty was an advance to a higher level of perception. This is the special significance of the famous opening lines of *Endymion:*

> A thing of beauty is a joy forever;
> Its loveliness increases; it will never
> Pass into nothingness.

This everlastingness in a thing of beauty, rather than the idea that beauty is truth, or the idea of the worship of beauty in itself, is the theme of the great *Ode on a Grecian Urn.* Never did poet strike the keynote of a poem more emphatically in his first lines; never did Keats use words with greater economy:

> Thou still unravish'd bride of quietness,
> Thou foster-child of silence and slow time,
> Sylvan historian.

Coming down through the centuries, unravished by time, adopted by time and silence, historian of the past, its creator long since forgotten, the urn and its decorations are eloquently illustrative of the permanency of beauty. . . . Not "truth" but "forever" is the key word; this poem is one of the superb examples in all literature for its expression in every image and every stanza of an abstract truth by imaginative suggestion, without overt assertion. The emotional reaction is also completely integrated with the idea of the poem.

The idea of the permanency of beauty leads directly to "the worship of the principle of beauty in all things," which is the central position with Keats. . . .

No. 43 Margaret Sherwood, *Undercurrents of Influence in English Romantic Poetry* (Cambridge, Massachusetts: Harvard University Press, 1934), 246.

In the *Ode on a Grecian Urn* there is little myth, but there is a master-stroke in the wonder at whose shrine among the gods those believers in the little town had gone to worship. It is one of the unanswered questions roused by the Ode; some god of compelling power, for all were gone.

No. 44   Claude Lee Finney, *The Evolution of Keats's Poetry,* Vol. II (Cambridge, Massachusetts: Harvard University Press, 1936), 636-645.

The *Ode on a Grecian Urn* follows closely and logically in thought after the *Ode on Melancholy.* Keats attempted to solve the problem of beauty and decay which caused his melancholy. Saddened by the mutability of natural beauty, he sought consolation in the more permanent beauty of art. The artist is a part of flowing nature, he knew, but the artist can arrest the fleeting beauty of nature and express it in the relatively eternal form of art. He became aware of this idea in 1817, when he was steeping himself in English poetry of the Renaissance. He read the boasts of sonneteers, such as Shakespeare, that the beauty of their mistresses would live forever in their powerful rhymes. He drew a clear distinction in *Endymion,* we have seen, between the beauty of nature and the beauty of art. And on June 26, 1818, while he was visiting the lakes and mountains of Westmoreland, he wrote his brother Tom:

> I shall learn poetry here and shall henceforth write more than ever, for the abstract endeavor of being able to add a mite to that mass of beauty which is harvested from these grand materials, by the finest spirits, and put into etherial existence for the relish of one's fellow.

Keats discussed poetry, painting, and sculpture with his friends, Haydon, Hazlitt, and Severn, and he learned to distinguish between the functions of these three arts. He may have been influenced, de Sélincourt suggested, by the sonnet which Wordsworth composed in 1811 upon sight of a picture which Sir George Beaumont had painted. . . . [See No. 3.]

As in the *Ode to a Nightingale* Keats contrasted the mortal world of pain, decay, and death with the immortal world of beauty and joy in which the nightingale sang, so in the *Ode on a Grecian Urn* he contrasted mortal life with the immortal life of art. The persons carved on the urn have advantages as well as limitations. They are held immovable and immortal in a moment of ecstatic endeavor. They cannot achieve the objects for which they strive, but they will not suffer the decay and death of mortal life. They feel passion more than human, but they will not have, like mortal men, the aftermath of passion—"a heart high-sorrowful and cloy'd, A burning forehead, and a parching tongue." . . .

The *Ode on a Grecian Urn* is a rich mosaic of Keats's experience in life and in art. The urn which he described is an imaginary urn which he intuited out of his recollections of various vases, friezes, paintings, and poems. He saw some vases, including the Townley Vase, in original form in the British Museum. . . .

The "leaf-fringed legend" in the first stanza refers to the fringe of leaves which is carved around the neck of many vases, the Sosibios Vase and the Borghese Vase, for example. The Bacchic throng with its "wild ecstasy" was suggested by the Townley Vase and the Borghese Vase. The "maiden loth," the "mad pursuit," and the "struggle to escape" were suggested by details in the Townley Vase. In one group in this vase a maenad is fleeing from a man who is pursuing. The "pipes and timbrels" were suggested by the Borghese Vase, on which a youth plays on pipes and a maiden shakes a timbrel over her head and left shoulder. "Tempe" was derived, as de Sélincourt pointed out, from Collins' ode *The Passions*. The Bacchic scenes on these vases reminded Keats of a similar scene in Collins' ode, in which Joy, playing on the pipe, inspired such ecstasy that they who heard the strain thought that they saw the maids of Tempe's vale dancing to some unwearied minstrel.

The description of the fair youth in the second stanza who is singing a song which he cannot leave beneath trees which will never be bare is a fusion of details which Keats remembered from vases and poetry. In the Borghese Vase there is a youth who is dancing and apparently singing; there are no trees but there is a fringe of leaves above his head. The trees which will never be bare were a reminiscence, however, of some verses in Shakespeare's sonnet 12. . . . The bold lover who cannot kiss his mistress, though winning near the goal, was suggested by a group in the Townley Vase in which a youth and a maiden in a half-embrace are on the point of kissing. . . .

In the *Ode on a Grecian Urn* Keats represented, as we have seen, two kinds of beauty in Greek life: the beauty of the Bacchic throng, a beauty of youth and energy and joy; and the beauty of the pastoral sacrifice, a beauty of clear serenity and quiet piety. He learned the beauty which he associated with Greek life from Greek sculpture, which he saw in fragmentary but original form, rather than from Greek poetry, which he read in warped and colored translations. He studied the Elgin Marbles with Haydon, who knew more about them than any other man in that age. He went to see these fragments again and again, gazing at them in a state of ecstasy. On one occasion Severn discovered him before the marbles, his "eyes shining so brightly" and his "face so lit up by some visionary rapture" that the painter stole quietly away without intruding. . . .

Keats began to appreciate the youth and the energy and the joy of Greek life in 1817 when he was viewing the Elgin Marbles with Haydon, studying Renaissance poetry, and composing *Endymion*. His appreciation of the quiet, radiant serenity of Greek life began at the end of 1818, when, oppressed by painful experience and stirred into a restless fever, he longed for serenity. The top of sovereignty, he said again and again in the letters and poems which he wrote in the first half of 1819, is to view circumstances in a calm state of mind, to behold the naked truths of life with temperate blood. The calm, stoical fortitude which he attained in April and May of 1819 is the truest phase of humanism in his whole poetic career.

The imaginary Grecian urn which Keats described is untrue, as Paul Wolters pointed out, to the pure conventions of Greek art. A Greek sculptor would no more think of mingling a Bacchic throng with a pious sacrifice than a Greek dramatist would think of mingling tragedy and comedy in a play. The vase which Keats described belongs in the tradition of the neo-Attic or Roman type of vase instead of in the tradition of the pure Attic type. He had a precedent for the incongruous scenes on his vase, however, in the scene which Sosibios, a sculptor of the late Greek or Roman period, carved on a vase. . . .

In the final stanza of the *Ode on a Grecian Urn* Keats's imagination shifted its ground again and considered the empirical message which the figures carved on the urn will give to one generation of men after another. . . . This final stanza is not so perfect as the other stanzas of the ode. The transitions in thought are not sufficiently clear and there is no strict correspondence between the units of thought and the metrical units of quatrain and two tercets. "Attic shape" and "Fair attitude" remind us of the artificial epithets of eighteenth-century poetry. "Brede," used in the sense of "embroidery," is too unusual to be a typical eighteenth-century word but it is a reminiscence of Collins' *Ode to Evening*.

The thought of the stanza is intelligible although it is not very clearly expressed. We can understand it best by considering it as the final stage, or the conclusion, of the thought of the preceding stanzas. . . .

A consciousness of reality intruded also into Keats's contemplation of the pastoral sacrifice, the second picture on the urn. The little town, whose inhabitants were attending the sacrifice, seemed silent and desolate. The artistic arrest of life seemed an infliction in the sphere of reality. . . .

At this point in the ode, as at the corresponding point in the *Ode to a Nightingale,* thoughts of reality came doubly strong and dissolved the artistic illusion which the carved figures on the urn had inspired in him. The word "desolate," like the word "forlorn," may have been the element which recalled him to reality. The final stanza represents his thoughts and feelings on his return to reality. When the artistic illusion was dissolved, the urn with its carved figures seemed cold, silent, and inanimate. . . .

The Grecian urn, which symbolizes artistic beauty, like the song of the nightingale, which symbolizes natural beauty, failed to give him surcease from the pain of reality. In the epistle which he wrote to Reynolds more than a year before he expressed the same thought in the same words. At that time his imagination was beginning to reveal to him the evil in nature. It revealed, in the first place, the flux of all natural things and, above all, the mutability of beauty. . . . And it revealed, in the second place, "an eternal fierce destruction" among natural creatures. . . . At that time, however, he could not find a satisfactory solution for the intuitions of evil which his imagination formed. . . .

Now, in May 1819, when he composed the *Ode on a Grecian Urn,* he had philosophized and he had learned the "lore of good and ill." He had perceived that evil, which is connected in natural creatures with egotistic instincts, is inherent and necessary in nature. He had discovered that he could not escape this evil by fleeing either into the world of natural beauty (the *Ode to a Nightingale*) or into the world of artistic beauty (the *Ode on a Grecian Urn*). He had learned, however, to endure evil with stoical fortitude and to look upon the naked truths of life with temperate blood. He had learned also that the egotistic instincts of natural creatures, which produce much of the evil in nature, are beautiful, that they are the very thing in which poetry consists. The figures in the Bacchic throng on the Grecian urn are animated by natural instincts. The bold lover pursues the fleeing maiden with the same instinctive eagerness with which a hawk or a stoat pursues its mate. These instinctive actions, Keats perceived, are true and they are beautiful. . . .

No. 45   F. R. Leavis, *Revaluation: Tradition and Development in English Poetry* (New York: George W. Stewart, 1947 [1936]), 252-254.

In fact, the main impulsion of the *Ode to a Nightingale* is essentially of the same order as that exhibited more simply by the *Ode on a Grecian Urn.* The urn, with its 'leaf-fringed legend,' gives a firmer stay to fancy than Keats could make of his imagined light-winged Dryad of the trees in its melodious plot of beechen green:

> Heard melodies are sweet, but those unheard
> Are sweeter . . .

—They are less disturbing, if less intensely felt. The compensation for the lack of rich immediacy is the idyllic serenity of the fourth stanza, with its 'green altar' and its 'peaceful citadel.' But even here we are made aware of a price to be paid. The serenity, before the end of the stanza, takes on another quality. . . . That 'emptied' is a key-word: we end the stanza contemplating, not the scene of ideally happy life, but the idea of streets that

> for evermore
> Will silent be,

and of a town to which

> not a soul to tell
> Why thou art desolate, can e'er return.

The victory over time seems an equivocal one. The attempt to get it both ways could, in the nature of things, have only a very qualified success.

Getting it both ways—the poem essentially *is* that. . . . Clearly, the urn for Keats is the incitement and support to a day-dream; the dream of a life that, without any drawbacks, shall give him all he desires—shall be for ever warm and still be enjoyed, remaining, 'among the leaves,' free from all the inevitable limitations that the nightingale, the light-winged Dryad, has never known.

These observations are not offered as proof of any remarkable percipience. The excuse for them is the puzzled, awed or Delphic attention that, in spite of their obviousness, has been paid to the famous concluding pronouncement of the Ode—the subtleties and profundities it still provides occasion for.

> 'Beauty is truth, truth beauty'—that is all
> Ye know on earth, and all ye need to know.

This surely, in the context just examined, should cause no metaphysical tremors of excitement or illumination, and needs no great profundity or ingenuity of any kind to elucidate it. The proposition is strictly in keeping with the attitude concretely embodied in the poem. The use of the word 'truth' corresponds strictly to the attitude towards reality analysed above. Life, alas! is not as we would have it; but it ought to be, and, with the aid of the Grecian urn, can be felt for a moment to be: imagination, concentrating on the beauty of the urn and ignoring the discordant and indocile facts, attains a higher reality, compared with which actual life seems thin and unreal. By the last stanza imagination in Keats has flagged, has relapsed from its inspired dream, the enchantment has waned and the actual has reasserted itself; but although the 'leaf-fringed legend' is now a 'Cold Pastoral,' it remains there, a permanent incitement to warm imaginings of an ideal life, a purely beautiful reality.

No. 46 Douglas Bush, *Mythology and the Romantic Tradition in English Poetry* (Cambridge, Massachusetts: Harvard University Press, 1937), 107-108.

At first sight Keats's theme in the *Ode to a Nightingale* and the *Ode on a Grecian Urn*—the two cannot be separated—is the belief that whereas the momentary experience of beauty is fleeting, the ideal embodiment of that moment in art, in song, or in marble, is an imperishable source of joy. If that were all, these odes should be hymns of triumph, and they are not. It is the very acme of melancholy that the joy he celebrates is joy in beauty that must die. Even when Keats proclaims that the song of the bird is immortal, that the sculptured lover feels an enduring love that is beyond the pains of human passion, his deepest emotions are fixed on the obverse side of his theme. He tries to believe, and with part of his mind he does believe and rejoice, in the immortality of ideal beauty, but he is too intense a lover of the here and now, of the human and tangible, to be satisfied by his own affirmations. It is the actual moment that is precious, that brings ecstasy with it, and the moment will not stay. The truth that Keats embraces is not that of his large humanitarian aspirations, nor the smaller measure of truth granted to the philosophic intellect, it is the truth, that is, the reality, apprehended through the senses. The author of these odes hears the still, sad music of humanity, but he tries to escape from it. The bird's song, poetry, carries him away from the lazar-house of life and above the level of the dull, perplexing brain; the urn is a symbol of untroubled beauty in the midst of human woe and it teases him out of thought. Was it the ecstasies and torments of love that intensified and decided the conflict, or was it that in poetry the senses had for the time won the victory and released him from the half-paralyzing claims of "higher" poetry? At any rate, as in *Endymion,* Keats is not wholly happy with the ideal, his instinct seeks the particular object and experience. And his instincts are more honest than Shelley's, for he is always aware of the cleavage in himself. He may grasp at the ideal as an authentic and inspiring sanction for his love of the actual, but he does not deceive himself, or us, when he endeavors, with more than Shelley's occasional misgivings, to bridge the gap between them. He cannot so easily rhapsodize about Intellectual Beauty when he is thinking of holding the hands of Harriet or Mary or Emilia or Jane. Neither beauty nor truth is for Keats a real abstraction, a Platonic Idea; beauty is something beautiful, the "material sublime." When he tries to generalize from a melancholy ecstasy, he remains at odds with himself. The urn is a joy for ever, but the marble figures are cold.

No. 47   D. G. James, *Scepticism and Poetry: An Essay on the Poetic Imagination* (London: Allen and Unwin, 1937), 9, 191-193.

I have sought . . . to emphasize that the imagination can never hope to free itself of scepticism; and that to claim that the imagination can give us what can be known for truth is an extravagance which cannot be upheld. It is for this reason that I have called the book *Scepticism and Poetry*. . . .

There has been a good deal of discussion concerning Keats' identification, in the *Ode on a Grecian Urn,* of beauty and truth. No doubt so bald an identification is meaningless, certainly too crude an expression for the purposes of his poem. . . . But apart from [A. C. Bradley's inadequate explanation, q.v.], it is more satisfactory to think that the clear explication of the saying is in the statement—'The imagination may be compared to Adam's dream—he awoke and found it truth.' . . . Is it likely, therefore, that in saying that Beauty is Truth, Keats is doing more than repeating, in more enigmatical form, what his remark about Adam's dream clearly conveys?—than saying that the dream of a transcendent object which commands the imagination is not an illusion? . . . The 'truth' for Keats was that 'essential beauty' which he calls the 'prototype' of all lovely things. Hence, when he says in his poem that Beauty is Truth . . . he is merely expressing his faith that 'Adam's dream' is a manisfestation, however obscure, of the highest reality. But to call it a faith is to say no more than that this ultimate hunger of the imagination can neither be satisfied nor eradicated.

This is so because . . . the imagination is unable to satisfy itself as to the reality of its supreme object. The 'dream' may indeed be only a dream. . . .

No. 48   Christopher Caudwell, *Illusion and Realty: A Study of the Sources of Poetry* (London: Macmillan, 1937), xiv, 99-100, 146-7.

One of the most brilliant of the Marxist critics, Caudwell states in his Introduction: "The criticism of art differs from pure enjoyment or creation in that it contains a *sociological* component. . . . There is only one sound sociology which lays bare the general active relation of the ideological products of society with each other and with concrete living—historical materialism. Historical materialism is therefore the basis of this study."

Keats is the first great poet to feel the strain of the poet's position in this stage of the bourgeois illusion, as producer for the free market. Wordsworth has a small income; Shelley . . . belongs to a rich family. . . . But Keats comes of a small bourgeois family and is always pestered by money problems. The sale of his poems is an important consideration to him.

. . . Keats' greater knowledge of bourgeois reality therefore led him to a position which was to set the keynote for future bourgeois poetry: "revolution" as a flight *from* reality. . . . The poet now escapes upon the "rapid wings of poesy" to a world of romance, beauty and sensuous life separate from the poor, harsh, real world of everyday life, which it sweetens and by its own loveliness silently condenms. . . . This other world is defiantly counterposed to the real world.

> "Beauty is truth, truth beauty"—that is all
> Ye know on earth, and all ye need to know.

And always it is threatened by stern reality in the shape of . . . the drab forces of everyday. . . .

. . . *Because* truth can only apply to reality . . . and because real concrete life is neither wholly subjective nor wholly objective but a dialectic active relation between the two (man's struggle with Nature), it is only these "impure" products of the struggle to which we can at all apply the criterion "true." Truth always has a social human reference—it means "true" in relation to man. Hence the criterion of mathematics, as Russell has pointed out, is never "truth," it is consistency. In the same way the criterion of music is "beauty." The fact that language in all its products contains a blend of both is because man in his real life is always actively striving to fulfil Keats' forecasts:

> Beauty is truth, truth beauty;

he is always struggling to make environment conform to instinct, consistency to beauty, and necessity to desire—in a word, to be free. . . . Consistency is the virtue of science, beauty of poetry— neither can ever become pure beauty or pure consistency, and yet it is their struggle to achieve this which drives on their development. Science yearns always towards mathematics, poetry towards music.

No. 49   G. St. Quintin, "The Grecian Urn," *Times Literary Supplement* (London, February 5, 1938), 92.

It is usual, I believe, to take the concluding couplet of Keats's "Ode to a Grecian Urn" as conveying the message of the Urn to mankind in general. . . .

An alternative suggestion is to assume that the "ye" of the last line is addressed to the figures on the Urn. For them Beauty *is* Truth because their experience is limited to the beautiful as depicted on the Urn. As Keats points out in the second and third stanzas, they would have none of the drawbacks of the ordinary course of experience. The Urn's message, if addressed to the world in general, and if literally interpreted, is absurd; but the Urn remains "a friend to man" because when he contemplates it he can escape from the real world to the world of imagination, where Beauty *is* Truth. This interpretation, of course, requires that only the words "Beauty is Truth, Truth Beauty" be printed in inverted commas, as in Professor de Sélincourt's edition.

No. 50   H. Buxton Forman and Maurice Buxton Forman, eds., *The Poetical Works and Other Writings of John Keats* (New York; Scribner's, 1939), III, 157n.

In regard to the two final lines the version of the Lamia volume is adopted [in this edition]. In the transcripts there are no turned commas; and in the *Annals* the two lines are thus:

> Beauty is Truth, Truth Beauty.—That is all
> Ye know on earth, and all ye need to know.

This seems to confirm the limitation of the Urn's moral to the five words indicated in the text; and, although I have not thought it worth while to note all the variations of pointing and capitalling of the *Annals* version, I find them very characteristic of Keats, and suggestive of accurate printing from a fair manuscript of his. But for this I should have been disposed to regard the words

> that is all
> Ye know on earth, and all ye need to know

as a part of the Urn's lesson, and not as the poet's personal comment.

No. 51   George Wilson Knight, *The Starlit Dome: Studies in the Poetry of Vision* (London: Methuen Press, 1941), 294-296.

The *Grecian Urn* serenely explores that eternity intrinsic to art, a smooth circularity and 'quietness' enclosing wild action and fierce desires of 'mad pursuit,' 'struggle to escape,' 'wild ecstasy,' to make a miniature of human life, with its desires and conflicts. These are captured in a frozen activity: the youth always about to kiss, the maiden never fading, with nature sharing in this artistic immortality in enjoyment of eternal spring. The ode concentrates on and expands that recurring tendency in Keats to image a poised form, a stillness suggesting motion, what might be called a 'tiptoe' effect. So the urn pipes inward and spiritual music in terms of a fusion of stillness and motion. This somehow explores the 'depth of things,' to recall a phrase from *Hyperion,* since the essence of love and indeed all action and life is desire, a projection not sharing the negation of satisfaction, the 'cloyed' and 'sorrowful' heart, the physical anguish. The main business of all art is precisely such a union of time and space as you have here: whether in using the spatial as rough material for vital, and therefore temporal, significance, as in architecture or sculpture; or in building a time-sequence of words or sounds into an architectural unity. We are again reminded of the river and dome in *Kubla Khan,* and indeed the choice of an urn with its smooth surface and circular form is not fortuitous: urns, like cars, are favourites of Keats from the start. Temporal and nature suggestion (in the various actions, 'leaf-fring'd legend,' 'boughs,' 'trodden weed') is subdued within the one still, dome-like harmony, which here breathes a life 'above' all 'human passion,' corresponding to the sublimated icy-sunshine of Coleridge's paradox-resolving palace. This blends into the other fusion of man and nature so exquisitely realized in all Keats's handling of Greek myth, here recurring in 'Tempe' and 'Arcady' delicately placed. Pagan piety again crowns these with 'sacrifice,' 'green altar,' and the heifer's 'silken flanks,' ritual tonings being strong in all the odes. When the 'little town' is pitied for its consequent emptiness, an inevitable disparity between art and life is hinted. . . . The problems involved 'tease us out of thought' like 'eternity': indeed they are problems expressly of eternity. In *Endymion* (III. 1-43) 'majestic' powers, set, as in *Kubla Khan,* above 'Fate,' the 'abysm-birth' of elements and 'feud' of 'nothing' and 'creation,' are *silent as a consecrated urn.'* So, though it be a 'cold pastoral'—the ode itself is far more philosophical, and in that sense colder, than the others—it remains a 'friend to man,' speaking, like all great art, like *Paradise Lost* or *Hamlet,* the same spirit-tones to generation after generation, a basic language of which individuals themselves are only transitory expressions. There is sweetness and bitterness in the conception. But to each generation it utters one assurance perhaps not to be grasped until the mind is teased *out* of thought into some wider comprehension: that the fusion of the spatial and temporal which conditions what we call 'beauty' is a penetration of essential being and therefore identical with 'truth.'

No. 52   Geoffrey Tillotson, *Essays in Criticism and Research* (Cambridge, England: Cambridge University Press, 1942), xiv-xv, 128-129.

[Mr. Tillotson is discussing the necessity for sound textual scholarship as the basis for literary criticism.] My second example is almost comic in the economy of its accomplishment. For generations critics were to be observed 'pinnacled dim in the intense inane,' interpreting the close of Keats's 'Ode on a Grecian Urn.' . . . The critics have spun beautiful cobwebs 'without substance or profit' out of those last two lines. In 1938, however, Mr G. St Quintin robbed them of much of their imaginary weft. He interpreted the obscurity as follows: [See No. 49.] Mr St Quintin's 'alternative suggestion' must be given its place in any discussion of the text of the poem. This is not the occasion for any such discussion, but it is already clear that Mr St Quintin's discovery helps to confirm the authority of the text of 'Poems' 1820. Unfortunately the latest edition prints the text as it appeared in 'The Annals of the Fine Arts,' a text which does not employ any quotation marks. If Keats were responsible for the text in the 'Annals,' it seems that he deliberately revised the pointing for 'Poems' 1820 in the hope, unfulfilled for over a century, that quotation marks would make his meaning clear. Mr St Quintin's understanding of the pointing, and therefore his discriminating of the choice of meanings for 'ye,' and therefore his choice of the better one—this chain of deduction has relieved Keats of a charge of pretentiousness which everything else he wrote renders him unlikely to have deserved. If the Ode cannot be allowed to end as well as it began and continued—the grammar of the close is not self-evident enough to be happy—Keats is at least found writing an admirable sense. . . . .

The word *brede* ([in Collins] 'Ode to Evening') has more certain sources than Milton's *braid* ('Comus') which Professor Ainsworth suggests. Milton had used the word in prose, and Dryden in his 'Essay on the Georgics' writes 'in a curious Brede of Needlework.' In poetry the first use seems that of Waller: 'On a Brede of Divers Colours' opens:

> Twice twenty slender virgin-fingers twine
> This curious web. . . .

Later, Philips in 'Cyder' (1708) uses 'watry brede' for the rainbow. Pope employs the word for Penelope's web ('Odyssey,' XIX, 179) and Akenside in 1744 follows Philips in applying it to the rainbow. The sense of the word seems sufficiently indicated from these three instances; it appears to have been Keats who confused the denotation (see 'Grecian Urn').

No. 53   Stephen A. Larrabee, *English Bards and Grecian Marbles: The Relationship Between Sculpture and Poetry Especially in the Romantic Period* (New York: Columbia University Press, 1943), 10 [major discussion, 221-225, not cited].

When a poet experiences sculpture emotionally and then re-creates it imaginatively in poetry, the specific works which stimulated his activity may recede into the background and become somewhat incidental. The "Ode on a Grecian Urn" is probably as close as any Romantic—or, for that matter, any English—poem to the ideal of poetic sculpture; yet even there Keats indulged his fondness for exhibiting his personal sensations in the cadenza-like departure from sculpture of the third stanza. In his envious rehearsal of the imagined "happy, happy love" of the figures on the urn, the poet almost lost sight of the actual object. The reader feels, however, that the cadenza of personal feeling represented an essential element in the sculptural quality which Keats had apprehended in gazing on Grecian urns and statues and, consequently, wished to convey in his poetic and imaginative re-creation.

No. 54   Herbert Marshall McLuhan, "Aesthetic Pattern in Keats's Odes," *University of Toronto Quarterly*, XII (January 1943), 177-178.

There are three basic themes involved in this ode, and they are of equal importance. The first is that of pastoral, with all its implications of rural and romantic peace and beauty. Pastoral offers a conventional escape for hearts "high-sorrowful and cloy'd"; the sophisticated have often cultivated it. The second theme, less explicit, is that of pagan culture under the sentimental aspect of its superiority to the current code—its freedom from complexity and dogma. Significantly, this conventional theme serves Keats's purpose in "discrediting" the urn as an escape; for "what maidens loth" and "that heifer lowing at the skies" strike a grim sacrificial note which is not to be mistaken. The third theme is also nostalgic: the life of aesthetic contemplation offered by the urn. In the artistic organization of the poem they are given alternate stress, and their tensions are relaxed in the last stanza by what can only be called an outright rejection of all three modes of escape.

No. 55 Kenneth Burke, "Symbolic Action in a Poem by Keats," [1943] *A Grammar of Motives* (New York: Prentice-Hall, 1952), 447-463.

Too long to quote in its entirety, Burke's essay sets out "to analyze the 'Ode on a Grecian Urn' as a viaticum that leads, by a series of transformations, into the oracle, 'Beauty is truth, truth beauty.' We shall analyze the Ode 'dramatistically,' in terms of symbolic action." At the end of his closely-argued analysis, Burke presents a summary of his essay; it is the summary (461-462) which is given here.

To review briefly: The poem begins with an ambiguous fever which in the course of the further development is "separated out," splitting into a bodily fever and a spiritual counterpart. The bodily passion is the malign aspect of the fever, the mental action its benign aspect. In the course of the development, the malign passion is transcended and the benign active partner, the intellectual exhilaration, takes over. At the beginning, where the two aspects were ambiguously one, the bodily passion would be the "scene" of the mental action (the "objective symptoms" of the body would be paralleled by the "subjective symptoms" of the mind, the bodily state thus being the other or ground of the mental state). But as the two become separated out, the mental action transcends the bodily passion. It becomes an act in its own right, making discoveries and assertions not grounded in the bodily passion. And this quality of action, in transcending the merely physical symptoms of the fever, would thus require a different ground or scene, one more suited in quality to the quality of the transcendent act.

The transcendent act is concretized, or "materialized," in the vision of the "immortal" scene, the reference in Stanza IV to the original scene of the Urn, the "heavenly" scene of a dead, or immortal, Greece (the scene in which the Urn was originally enacted and which is also fixed on its face). . . . We suggested that the poet is here coming upon a new internal sky, through identification with the Urn as act, the same sky that he came upon through identification with the enactments of Chapman's translation.

This transcendent scene is the level at which the earthly laws of contradiction no longer prevail. Hence, in the terms of this scene, he can proclaim the unity of truth and beauty (of science and art), a proclamation which he needs to make precisely because here was the basic split responsible for the romantic agitation (in both poetic and philosophic idealism). That is, it was gratifying to have the oracle proclaim the unity of poetry and science because the values of technology and business were causing them to be at odds. And from the perspective of a "higher level" (the perspective of a dead or immortal scene transcending the world of temporal contradictions) the split could be proclaimed once more a unity.

At this point, at this stage of exaltation, the fever has been replaced by chill. But the bodily passion has completely dropped out of account. All is now mental action. Hence, the chill (as in the ecstatic exclamation, "Cold Pastoral!") is proclaimed only in its benign aspect.

No. 56   Yvor Winters, *In Defense of Reason* (New York: The Swallow Press & William Morrow and Co., 1947), 475-476. [From *The Anatomy of Nonsense* (New Directions, 1943)].

Like Eliot, I find the statement of Keats a blemish, and for the reason given. . . . The difficulty in the statement by Keats, however, is not the same difficulty that Dante might be supposed to encounter in Lucretius or Lucretius in Dante; the difficulty is one of simple incomprehensibility. Beauty and Truth are abstract terms with distinct meanings; to say that they are interchangeable without explaining oneself leads to confusion. . . .

No. 57   Cleanth Brooks, "Keats's Sylvan Historian: History without Footnotes," [1943] *The Well Wrought Urn: Studies in the Structure of Poetry* (New York: Reynal and Hitchcock, 1947), 140-152.

. . . the poem itself is obviously intended to be a parable on the nature of poetry, and of art in general. The "Ode" has apparently been an enigmatic parable, to be sure. . . . The very ambiguity of the statement, "Beauty is truth, truth beauty" ought to warn us against insisting very much on the statement in isolation, and to drive us back to a consideration of the context in which the statement is set.

It will not be sufficient, however, if it merely drives us back to a study of Keats's reading, his conversation, his letters. . . . The reason should be clear: our specific question is not what did Keats the man perhaps want to assert here about the relation of beauty and truth; it is rather: was Keats the poet able to exemplify that relation in this particular poem? . . .

Now, suppose that one could show that Keats's lines . . . constitute a speech, a consciously riddling paradox, put in the mouth
of a particular character, and modified by the total context of
the poem. If we could demonstrate that the speech was "in character," was dramatically appropriate, was properly prepared for
. . . should we not have waived the question of the scientific or
philosophic truth of the lines in favor of the application of a
principle curiously like that of dramatic propriety? I suggest that
some such principle is the only one legitimately to be invoked in
any case. Be this as it may, the "Ode on a Grecian Urn" provides
us with as neat an instance as one could wish in order to test the
implications of such a maneuver.

It has seemed best to be perfectly frank about procedure: the
poem is to be read in order to see whether the last lines of the
poem are not, after all, dramatically prepared for. Yet there are
some claims to be made upon the reader too, claims which he, for
his part, will have to be prepared to honor. He must not be
allowed to dismiss the early characterizations of the urn as merely
so much vaguely beautiful description. He must not be too much
surprised if "mere decoration" turns out to be meaningful symbolism—or if ironies develop where he has been taught to expect
only sensuous pictures. Most of all, if the teasing riddle spoken
finally by the urn is not to strike him as a bewildering break in
tone, he must not be too much disturbed to have the element of
paradox latent in the poem emphasized, even in those parts of
the poem which have none of the energetic crackle of wit with
which he usually associates paradox. This is surely not too much
to ask of the reader—namely, to assume that Keats meant what he
said and that he chose his words with care. After all, the poem
begins on a note of paradox, though a mild one: for we ordinarily
do not expect an urn to speak at all; and yet, Keats does more
than this: he begins his poem by emphasizing the apparent
contradiction.

The silence of the urn is stressed—it is a "bride of quietness";
it is a "foster-child of silence," but the urn is a "historian" too.
Historians tell the truth, or are at least expected to tell the truth.
What is a "Sylvan historian"? A historian who is like the forest
rustic, a woodlander? Or, a historian who writes histories of the
forest? Presumably, the urn is sylvan in both senses. True, the
latter meaning is uppermost: the urn can "express / A flowery tale
more sweetly than our rhyme," and what the urn goes on to
express is a "leaf-fring'd legend" of "Tempe or the dales of
Arcady." But the urn, like the "leaf-fring'd legend" which it

tells, is covered with emblems of the fields and forests: "Over-wrought, / With forest branches and the trodden weed." When we consider the way in which the urn utters its history, the fact that it must be sylvan in both senses is seen as inevitable. Perhaps too the fact that it is a rural historian, a rustic, a peasant his-torian, qualifies in our minds the dignity and the "truth" of the histories which it recites. Its histories, Keats has already conceded, may be characterized as "tales"—not formal history at all.

The sylvan historian certainly supplies no names and dates—"What men or gods are these?" the poet asks. What it does give is action—of men *or* gods, of godlike men or of superhuman (though not daemonic) gods—action, which is not the less intense for all that the urn is cool marble. The words "mad" and "ecstasy" occur, but it is the quiet, rigid urn which gives the dynamic picture. And the paradox goes further: the scene is one of violent love-making, a Bacchanalian scene, but the urn itself is like a "still unravish'd bride," or like a child, a child "of silence and slow time." It is not merely like a child, but like a "foster-child." The exactness of the term can be defended. "Silence and slow time," it is suggested, are not the true parents, but foster-parents. They are too old, one feels, to have borne the child themselves. Moreover, they dote upon the "child" as grandparents do. The urn is fresh and un-blemished; it is still young, for all its antiquity, and time which destroys so much has "fostered" it.

With Stanza II we move into the world presented by the urn, into an examination, not of the urn as a whole—as an entity with its own form—but of the details which overlay it. But as we enter that world, the paradox of silent speech is carried on, this time in terms of the objects portrayed on the vase.

The first lines of the stanza state a rather bold paradox—even the dulling effect of many readings has hardly blunted it. At least we can easily revive its sharpness. Attended to with care, it is a statement which is preposterous, and yet true—true on the same level on which the original metaphor of the speaking urn is true. The unheard music is sweeter than any audible music. The poet has rather cunningly enforced his conceit by using the phrase, "ye soft pipes." . . . Yet, by characterizing the pipes as "soft," the poet has provided a sort of realistic basis for his metaphor: the pipes, it is suggested, are playing very softly; if we listen carefully, we can hear them; their music is just below the threshold of normal sound.

This general paradox runs through the stanza: action goes on though the actors are motionless; the song will not cease; the lover cannot leave his song; the maiden, always to be kissed, never actually kissed, will remain changelessly beautiful. . . .

The poet is obviously stressing the fresh, unwearied charm of the scene itself which can defy time and is deathless. But, at the same time, the poet is being perfectly fair to the terms of his metaphor. The beauty portrayed is deathless because it is lifeless. And it would be possible to shift the tone easily and ever so slightly by insisting more heavily on some of the phrasings so as to give them a darker implication. Thus, in the case of "thou canst not leave / Thy song," one could interpret: the musician cannot leave the song even if he would: he is fettered to it, a prisoner. In the same way, one could enlarge on the hint that the lover is not wholly satisfied and content: "never canst thou kiss, / . . . *yet, do not grieve.*" These items are mentioned here, not because one wishes to maintain that the poet is bitterly ironical, but because it is important for us to see that even here the paradox is being used fairly, particularly in view of the shift in tone which comes in the next stanza.

This third stanza represents, as various critics have pointed out, a recapitulation of earlier motifs. The boughs which cannot shed their leaves, the unwearied melodist, and the ever-ardent lover reappear. Indeed, I am not sure that this stanza can altogether be defended against the charge that it represents a falling-off from the delicate but firm precision of the earlier stanzas. There is a tendency to linger over the scene sentimentally: the repetition of the word "happy" is perhaps symptomatic of what is occurring. Here, if anywhere, in my opinion, is to be found the blemish on the ode—not in the last two lines. Yet, if we are to attempt a defense of the third stanza, we shall come nearest success by emphasizing the paradoxical implications of the repeated items; for whatever development there is in the stanza inheres in the increased stress on the paradoxical element. . . .

The paradox is carried further in the case of the lover whose love is "For ever warm and still to be enjoy'd." We are really dealing with an ambiguity here, for we can take "still to be enjoy'd" as an adjectival phrase on the same level as "warm"—that is, "still virginal and warm." But the tenor of the whole poem suggests that the warmth of the love depends upon the fact that it has not been enjoyed—that is, "warm and still to be enjoy'd" may mean also "warm *because* still to be enjoy'd."

. . . Garrod, sensing this ironic undercurrent, seems to interpret it as an element over which Keats was not able to exercise full control. . . . Keats's attitude, even in the early stanzas, is more complex than Garrod would allow: it is more complex and more ironic, and a recognition of this is important if we are to be able to relate the last stanza to the rest of the "Ode." Keats is perfectly aware that the frozen moment of loveliness is more dynamic than is the fluid world of reality *only* because it is frozen. The love depicted on the urn remains warm and young because it is not human flesh at all but cold, ancient marble.

With Stanza IV, we are still within the world depicted by the urn, but the scene presented in this stanza forms a contrast to the earlier scenes. It emphasizes, not individual aspiration and desire, but communal life. It constitutes another chapter in the history that the "Sylvan historian" has to tell. And again, names and dates have been omitted. We are not told to what god's altar the procession moves, nor the occasion of the sacrifice. . . .

The stanza has been justly admired. Its magic of effect defies reduction to any formula. Yet, without pretending to "account" for the effect in any mechanical fashion, one can point to some of the elements active in securing the effect: there is the suggestiveness of the word "green" in "green altar"—something natural, spontaneous, living; there is the suggestion that the little town is caught in a curve of the seashore, or nestled in a fold of the mountains—at any rate, is something secluded and something naturally related to its terrain; there is the effect of the phrase "peaceful citadel," a phrase which involves a clash between the ideas of war and peace and resolves it in the sense of stability and independence without imperialistic ambition—the sense of stable repose.

But to return to the larger pattern of the poem: Keats does something in this fourth stanza which is highly interesting in itself and thoroughly relevant to the sense in which the urn is a historian. One of the most moving passages in the poem is that in which the poet speculates on the strange emptiness of the little town which, of course, has not been pictured on the urn at all. . . .

If one attends closely to what Keats is doing here, he may easily come to feel that the poet is indulging himself in an ingenious fancy, an indulgence, however, which is gratuitous and finally silly; that is, the poet has created in his own imagination the town implied by the procession of worshipers, has given it a special character of desolation and loneliness, and then has gone on to treat it as if it were a real town to which a stranger might actually come and be puzzled by its emptiness. . . . But, actually, of course, no one will ever discover the town except by the very same process by which Keats has discovered it: namely, through the figured urn, and then, of course, he will not need to ask why it is empty. . . .

It will not be too difficult, however, to show that Keats's extension of the fancy is not irrelevant to the poem as a whole. The "reality" of the little town has a very close relation to the urn's character as a historian. If the earlier stanzas have been concerned with such paradoxes as the ability of static carving to convey dynamic action, of the soundless pipes to play music sweeter than that of the heard melody, of the figured lover to have a love more warm and panting than that of breathing flesh and blood, so in the same way the town implied by the urn comes to have a richer and more important history than that of actual cities. Indeed, the imagined town is to the figured procession as the unheard melody is to the carved pipes of the unwearied melodist. And the poet, by pretending to take the town as real—so real that he can imagine the effect of its silent streets upon the stranger who chances to come into it—has suggested in the most powerful way possible its essential reality for him—and for us. It is a case of the doctor's taking his own medicine: the poet is prepared to stand by the illusion of his own making.

With Stanza V we move back out of the enchanted world portrayed by the urn to consider the urn itself once more as a whole, as an object. The shift in point of view is marked with the first line of the stanza by the apostrophe, "O Attic shape . . ." It is the urn itself as a formed thing, as an autonomous world, to which the poet addresses these last words. And the rich, almost breathing world which the poet has conjured up for us contracts and hardens into the decorated motifs on the urn itself: "with brede / Of marble men and maidens overwrought." The beings who have a life above life—"All breathing human passion far above"—are marble, after all.

This last is a matter which, of course, the poet has never denied. The recognition that the men and maidens are frozen, fixed, arrested, has, as we have already seen, run through the second, third, and fourth stanzas as an ironic undercurrent. The central paradox of the poem, thus, comes to conclusion in the phrase, "Cold Pastoral." The word "pastoral" suggests warmth, spontaneity, the natural and the informal as well as the idyllic, the simple, and the informally charming. What the urn tells is a "flowery tale," a "leaf-fring'd legend," but the "sylvan historian" works in terms of marble. The urn itself is cold, and the life beyond life which it expresses is life which has been formed, arranged. The urn itself is a "silent form," and it speaks, not by means of statement, but by "teasing us out of thought." It is as enigmatic as eternity is, for, like eternity, its history is beyond time, outside time, and for this very reason bewilders our time-ridden minds: it teases us.

The marble men and maidens of the urn will not age as flesh-and-blood men and women will: "When old age shall this generation waste." . . . The marble men and women lie outside time. The urn which they adorn will remain. The "Sylvan historian" will recite its history to other generations.

What will it say to them? Presumably, what it says to the poet now: that "formed experience," imaginative insight, embodies the basic and fundamental perception of man and nature. The urn is beautiful, and yet its beauty is based—what else is the poem concerned with?—on an imaginative perception of essentials. Such a vision is beautiful but it is also true. The sylvan historian presents us with beautiful histories, but they are true histories, and it is a good historian.

Moreover, the "truth" which the sylvan historian gives is the only kind of truth which we are likely to get on this earth, and, furthermore, it is the only kind that we *have* to have. The names, dates, and special circumstances, the wealth of data—these the sylvan historian quietly ignores. But we shall never get all the facts anyway—there is no end to the accumulation of facts. Moreover, mere accumulations of facts—a point our own generation is only beginning to realize—are meaningless. The sylvan historian does better than that: it takes a few details and so orders them that we have not only beauty but insight into essential truth. Its "history," in short, is a history without footnotes. It has the validity of myth—not myth as a pretty but irrelevant make-belief, an idle fancy, but myth as a valid perception into reality.

So much for the "meaning" of the last lines of the "Ode." It is an interpretation which differs little from past interpretations. It is put forward here with no pretension to novelty. What is important is the fact that it can be derived from the context of the "Ode" itself.

. . . If we can see that the assertions made in a poem are to be taken as part of an organic context, if we can resist the temptation to deal with them in isolation, then we may be willing to go on to deal with the world-view, or "philosophy," or "truth" of the *poem as a whole* in terms of its dramatic wholeness: that is, we shall not neglect the maturity of attitude, the dramatic tension, the emotional *and* intellectual coherence in favor of some statement of theme abstracted from it by paraphrase. Perhaps, best of all, we might learn to distrust our ability to represent any poem adequately by paraphrase. Such a distrust is healthy. Keats's sylvan historian, who is not above "teasing" us, exhibits such a distrust, and perhaps the point of what the sylvan historian "says" is to confirm us in our distrust.

No. 58 James Ralston Caldwell, *John Keats' Fancy: The Effect on Keats of the Psychology of His Day* (Cornell University Press, 1945), 162-173, 183-190.

The subtitle of this important study indicates its subject. Students of literature have become more and more persuaded (with some notable exceptions) that the study of poetry, particularly of poetry of the romantic period, requires the fullest understanding possible of the intellectual and personal milieu in which the poet lived and wrote. Thus, writes Mr. Caldwell, "It is the purpose of this book to show that ideas derived from the psychology of his day were of radical importance in Keats's creative life, to observe how these ideas affected his work-ways, and thus better to understand his poetry." (pp. 7-8)

No. 59 Aldous Huxley, *The Perennial Philosophy* (New York: Harper and Brothers, 1945), 125, 137-138.

In religious literature the word "truth" is used indiscriminately in at least three distinct and very different senses. Thus, it is sometimes treated as a synonym for "fact," as when it is affirmed that God is Truth—meaning that He is the primordial Reality. But this is clearly not the meaning of the word in such a phrase as "worshipping God in spirit and in truth." Here, it is obvious, "truth" signifies direct apprehension of spiritual Fact, as opposed to second-hand knowledge *about* Reality, formulated in sentences and accepted on authority or because an argument from previously granted postulates was logically convincing. And finally there is the more ordinary meaning of the word, as in such a sentence as, "This statement is the truth," where we mean to assert that the verbal symbols of which the statement is composed correspond to the facts to which it refers. . . .

"Beauty is truth, truth, beauty." But unfortunately Keats failed to specify in which of its principal meanings he was using the word "truth." Some critics have assumed that he was using it in the third of the senses listed at the opening of this section, and have therefore dismissed the aphorism as nonsensical. $Zn + H_2SO_4 = ZnSO_4 + H_2$. This is a truth in the third sense of the word—and, manifestly, this truth is not identical with beauty. But no less manifestly Keats was not talking about this kind of "truth." He was using the word primarily in its first sense, as a synonym for "fact," and secondarily with the significance attached to it in the Johannine phrase, "to worship God in truth." His sentence, therefore, carries two meanings. "Beauty is the Primordial Fact, and the Primordial Fact is Beauty, the principle of all particular beauties"; and "Beauty is an immediate experience, and this immediate experience is identical with Beauty-as-Principle, Beauty-as-Primordial-Fact." The first of these statements is fully in accord with the doctrines of the Perennial Philosophy. . . .

With Keats's statement in its secondary meaning the exponents of the Perennial Philosophy would certainly disagree. The experience of beauty in art or in nature may be qualitatively akin to the immediate, unitive experience of the divine Ground or Godhead; but it is not the same as that experience, and the particular beauty-fact experienced, though partaking in some sort of the divine nature, is at several removes from the Godhead. The poet, the nature lover, the aesthete are granted apprehensions of Reality analogous to those vouchsafed to the selfless contemplative; but because they have not troubled to make themselves perfectly selfless, they are incapable of knowing the divine Beauty in its fulness, as it is in itself. The poet is born with the capacity of arranging words in such a way that something of the quality of the graces and inspirations he has received can make itself felt to other human beings in the white spaces, so to speak, between the lines of his verse. This is a great and precious gift; but if the poet remains content with his gift, if he persists in worshipping the beauty in art and nature without going on to make himself capable, through selflessness, of apprehending Beauty as it is in the divine Ground, then he is only an idolater. True, his idolatry is among the highest of which human beings are capable; but an idolatry, none the less, it remains.

No. 60 Allen Tate, "A Reading of Keats," [1945] *On the Limits of Poetry* (New York: Swallow, 1948), 177-180.

If we glance at "Ode on a Grecian Urn," we shall see Keats trying to unify his pictorial effects by means of direct philosophical statement. "Do I wake or sleep?" at the end of the Nightingale ode asks the question: Which is reality, the symbolic nightingale or the common world? The famous Truth-Beauty synthesis at the end of the "Grecian Urn" contains the same question, but this time it is answered. As Mr. Kenneth Burke sees it, Truth is the practical scientific world and Beauty is the ideal world above change. The "frozen" figures on the urn, being both dead and alive, constitute a scene which is at once perceptible and fixed. "This transcendent scene," says Mr. Burke, "is the level at which the earthly laws of contradiction no longer prevail." . . . Much of the little that I know about this poem I have learned from Mr. Burke and from Mr. Cleanth Brooks, who have studied it more closely than any other critics; and what I am about to say will sound ungrateful. I suspect that the dialectical solution is Mr. Burke's rather than Keats's, and that Mr. Brooks "irony" and "dramatic propriety" are likewise largely his own. . . . . I find myself agreeing with Mr. Middleton Murry . . . who admits that the statement is out of place "in the context of the poem itself." I would point to a particular feature, in the last six lines of stanza four, which I feel that neither Mr. Burke nor Mr. Brooks has taken into a certain important kind of consideration. Here Keats tells us that in the background of this world of eternal youth there is another, from which it came, and that this second world has thus been emptied and is indeed a dead world. . . . Mr. Burke quite rightly sees in this passage the key to the symbolism of the entire poem. It is properly the "constatation" of the tensions of the imagery. What is the meaning of this perpetual youth on the urn? One of its meanings is that it is perpetually anti-youth and anti-life; it is in fact dead, and "can never return." Are we not faced again with the same paradox we had in the Nightingale ode, that the intensest life is achieved in death? Mr. Burke brings out with great skill the erotic equivalents of the life-death symbols. . . . Yet I feel that Mr. Burke's own dialectical skill leads him to consider the poem, when he is through with it, a philosophical discourse; but it is, if it is anything (and it is a great deal), what is ordinarily known as a work of art. Mr. Burke's elucidation of the Truth-Beauty proposition in the last stanza is the most convincing dialectically that I have seen; but Keats did not write Mr. Burke's elucidation; and I feel that the entire last stanza, except the phrase "Cold Pastoral" (which probably ought to be somewhere else in the poem) is an illicit commentary added by the poet to a "meaning" which was symbolically complete at the end of the preceding stanza, number four. Or perhaps it may be said that Keats did to some extent write Mr. Burke's elucidation; that is why I feel that the final stanza (though magnificently written) is redundant and out of form. . . .

No. 61 Victor M. Hamm, "Keats' ODE ON A GRECIAN URN, lines 49-50," *The Explicator,* III (May, 1945), 56.

I suggest as a possible reading of the lines in question: The urn seems to say, to the man contemplating it, "Beauty is truth, truth beauty." The poet comments: "That is all you know about the urn, and all you need to know." This reading would obviate the disturbance of the harmony of the poem . . . and it is justified by the series of unanswered questions in stanzas 1 and 4. . . . These questions, says the poet in his comment, . . . will never be answered on earth; but the urn's message, that artistic beauty is a kind of truth, and that truth is beautiful (a truism from Plato to Goethe and beyond), is all you know and all you need to know about it, since the urn's value is that of a work of art, not that of a historic document or monument.

No. 62   Roy P. Basler, "Keats' ODE ON A GRECIAN URN," *The Explicator*, IV (Oct. 1945), 6.

Mr. Hamm's explication . . . is without doubt correct in construing the comment following the quotation marks as the poet's, but seems to me to depart from the text in supposing that it is addressed directly to the reader. Since the urn is addressed in the first line, and throughout the poem, why suppose a shift at the end? It seems to me that the poet's comment is thus: "That is all you (. . . 'sylvan historian') know, and all you need to know; but, I know a great deal more, and a different quality of beauty and truth." . . .

Both this ode and the "Ode to a Nightingale" renounce the anodyne of "romantic" beauty. . . . T. S. Eliot and J. M. Murry, as well as some other critics, have condemned what they do not take the trouble to understand. . . . At any rate, I see no "baffling paradox" in the idea that although the poet comprehends the message of the urn he does not find it sound philosophy in a world of things called real. . . .

No. 63   Josephine Miles, *Major Adjectives in English Poetry From Wyatt to Auden* (Berkeley and Los Angeles: University of California Press, 1946), 374-378.

Keats participated fully in the tradition of magnificence of adjectival quantity, quality, and structure. Like Spenser, Milton, and Collins, he used twelve adjectives to ten lines. Like all but Donne's, at least 60 per cent were descriptive qualifying adjectives. Like Spenser, Milton, Collins, Wordsworth, he used only half as many quantity terms, the terms of natural speech, as did the rest. Like Milton and Collins alone he stressed the past-participial modifier, the describable state. Like Milton and Collins too, and Tennyson, he used among his descriptive terms sheer sense terms in a proportion of a third, six times Wyatt's and Donne's and even three times Spenser's. His use of negative epithets is less than any but Tennyson's. . . .

The content of Keats' adjectives is by now very familiar to us. Of the major eleven, *fair, good, great,* and *sweet* were major for most others too, all through; *high* was characteristically Spenserian and Miltonic, and *little* and *old* were both Elizabethan and Romantic. Keats was thus somewhat more conventional than Collins. On the other hand, his *soft, green, golden* stem from the school of Pope, Collins, and Gray, and are the last instances of these three major emphases; and his *bright* he shares only with men of his own time, Wordsworth, Shelley, Emerson. His main emphasis, then, is both part of a long tradition and part of his own time. . . .

The top level of Keats' usage contains more adjectives than usual, and his secondary list is close, containing gentle and happy, deep, silver, white, wide, young. The presence of four colors in the two lists, and the relegation of the emotion terms to the secondary one, together characterize his emphasis, in his whole area of adjective reference, upon sense and especially sight. There is in him less of the named interplay between quality and feeling than in Milton and Collins. His major epithets do modify mood, and cheer, and pain, and passions and delights; but, much more often, music, day, service, luxuries, weather, path, array, abyss, sun, star, moon, roses, faces, lids, wings, stags, lakes, island, hill, turf, berries, doors, noises, flowers, rills, thunder, wine, Thames, Triton, wind, rustle, bloom, and song. Here is a world devoted to sense far more thoroughly than any heretofore; even the world of Collins paraded its abstractions through a scantier sensable realm. All these nouns described by Keats' major adjectives are the naturally accepted furniture of poetry since his time; it is therefore interesting to note how long it took even the strongest adjectival poetry to use this furniture; for Spenser and Milton and even Collins, still, fair, sweet, great, and soft were as often used with abstractions as with things. The greatest homogeneity, the greatest narrowing and centering of interest, seems to me visible on this upper level of Keats' usage. The stories, personages, judgments fall away, and a soft bright sweet physical world of scene remains. The main term closest to standard, the word *good,* Keats uses not to judge by, but colloquially: good man, good Knight, good Heavens! good gods! in accepted phrases.

In keeping with such concentration he makes few negative judgments, uses few *evils* and *cruels.* . . . One special kind is characteristic, however, the noting of absence in noiseless, tuneless, voiceless, soundless, [etc.] . . .

The adjectives of the Grecian Urn—unravish'd, slow, sylvan, flowery, leaf-fring'd, loth, mad, wild; then heard, sweet, unheard, sweeter, soft, sensual, endear'd, fair, bare, bold, winning, fair; then happy, happy, happy, unwearied, piping, new, happy, happy, happy, warm, panting, young, breathing, human, high-sorrowful, cloy'd, burning, parching; then coming, green, mysterious, lowing, silken, drest, little, sea, mountain-built, peaceful, pious, little, silent, desolate; then Attic, fair, marble, overwrought, forest, trodden, silent, Cold, old, other, all, all—bring in their course and their stanzaic grouping the conflict, rapture, excess, relief, and resolution in suspension which are the poem as any reader reads it, or even as Kenneth Burke reads it. In Cold Pastoral! too, we have a sign of the great power and position of the adjective for Keats: adjective and exclamation mark go together for him. . . .

So close the adjective seems to pure expressive form for Keats that we may justly identify his poetry with it . . . "A brighter word than bright, a fairer word than fair," was the unreachable goal of Keats' poetic spirit, which, while it was unsatisfied with epithet and asked for a more ineffable naming, asked still in the major terms, a *brighter* and a *fairer*.

No. 64 Werner W. Beyer, *Keats and the Daemon King* (New York: Oxford, 1947), 257-262.

Beyer finds the influence of the German poet Wieland (1733-1813) everywhere in Keats, and attempts to reinterpret the latter's poems in the light of the presumed "influence" of the former. Much as Weller, two decades before, had over-argued the importance of Mary Tighe in Keats, so Beyer in the case of Wieland. But many of the author's insights are in no way invalidated by his over-emphasis.

No. 65 Richard Church, *John Keats: An Introduction and a Selection* (London: Phoenix House, 1948), xv-xvi.

Goethe said 'continue to think and to find, to compose and to write, without letting others disturb you. A man must write as he lives.' Therefore he must first live equably, seeking a serene mind that shall be a smooth mirror reflecting everything, the horrors as well as the lights. He must come to a door over which he reads, 'Abandon hope, all ye who enter here,' and he must enter calmly without a heightened pulse. In that way the poet and the scientist are identified. The poet disregards all loss of hope because he is wholly concerned with the present, penetrating it and proving it to be eternity and therefore continent of truth's whole drama, and through that wholeness a pattern of beauty. Maybe this is what Keats meant by those much discussed lines at the end of the ode *On A Grecian Urn*.

No. 66   Samuel C. Chew, "The Nineteenth Century and After," *A Literary History of England,* ed. A. C. Baugh (New York: Appleton—Century-Crofts, 1948), 1249.

. . . *Ode on a Grecian Urn* where another contrast is developed, that of the permanence of art with the fleetingness of human passion. For all its beauty this ode is not quite flawless (the flaw is in stanza v; the ugly repetition of sound in "O Attic shape! Fair attitude!"), and the oft-quoted conclusion is open to the charge of ambiguity.

No. 67   Lord Gorell, *John Keats: The Principle of Beauty* (London: 1948), 81.

Not the first to do so, Lord Gorell points out the parallels between the Ode and Keats' verse letter to Reynolds, No. 58, written at Teignmouth, 25 March 1818. I cite below the relevant passages, some of which are often used by Keats scholars in interpreting the Ode.

> Dear Reynolds, as last night I lay in bed,
> There came before my eyes that wonted thread
> Of shapes, and shadows, and remembrances,
> That every other minute vex and please. . . .   4
> Some Titian colours touch'd into real life,—   19
> The sacrifice goes on; the pontiff knife
> Gleams in the Sun, the milk-white heifer lows,
> The pipes go shrilly, the libation flows: . . .   22
> O that our dreamings all, of sleep or wake,   67
> Would all their colours from the sunset take:
> From something of material sublime,
> Rather than shadow our own soul's day-time
> In the dark void of night. For in the world
> We jostle,—but my flag is not unfurl'd
> On the Admiral-staff,—and so philosophize
> I dare not yet! Oh, never will the prize,
> High reason, and the love of good or ill,
> Be my award! Things cannot to the will
> Be settled, but they tease us out of thought;
> Or is it that imagination brought
> Beyond its proper bound, yet still confin'd
> Lost in a sort of Purgatory blind,
> Cannot refer to any standard law
> Of either earth or heaven? It is a flaw
> In happiness, to see beyond our bourn,—
> It forces us in summer skies to mourn,
> It spoils the singing of the Nightingale.   85

No. 68 Richard Harter Fogle, *The Imagery of Keats and Shelley: A Comparative Study* (University of North Carolina Press, 1949), 172-177.

The *Ode on a Grecian Urn* is Keats's consummate expression of emphatic feeling and thought. In it empathy arises from prolonged and passionate contemplation of a beautiful object and is refined into aesthetic emotion, which in turn is expanded and uplifted into more comprehensive perceptions culminating in the Platonic merging of Beauty and Truth at the end of the poem. This refining and sublimating process is the result of the action upon empathy of another element, the "spectator" attitude—the calm detachment. . . . The relations of these two elements in the poem present themselves as a steady movement of advance into the object and withdrawal from it. . . .

The commencement of the *Ode* is muted, chaste, and cold. . . . The severe and simple harmonies of the vase do not easily yield up their secret. . . . But Keats begins to respond to its slowly disclosed invitation . . . as the measured movement of line and pattern beckons him inward. (11. 8-10.) The flat figures take on dimension and life, a perspective unrolls before him. . . . To his eyes all is at first generalized: men and maidens, excited movement and sound, ecstasy. The import of it all is not immediately clear.

Soon, however, the meaning of the figures reveals itself more fully. Caught up by a dynamic sense of motion, he enters into the feelings of the lover. Yet he is perfectly conscious of the difference between life and art, and this very consciousness invokes a new, complex emotion. (11. 17-20) The lover is betrayed by art; he is forever imprisoned in a timeless frustration. [But] . . . his love will be present always, and always fair. Cold comfort, one would unthinkingly say; but this eternity of aesthetic contemplation is the highest glory of art.

. . . This [third] stanza extends and enlarges the suggestions of stanza two. . . . He experiences warmth, he pants; he consummates his love, and goes on to the inevitable human aftermath of "A burning forehead, and a parching tongue." With this line the tide of empathy reaches its height in the poem; yet inseparable from it is the realization that these physical experiences are precisely what do not happen and could not happen. For the figures of the vase are contained forever in another medium than life.

The calmer tone of stanza four is indicative of a steady, progressive withdrawal. . . . Keats is still within the picture, or more aptly, on the actor's side of the proscenium arch. . . . With the paradox of the village, forever deserted because its inhabitants

have been spirited away by the magic pipings of art, he steps outside the frame of the proscenium arch once more. In stanza five
he is outside, reflecting upon what he has experienced.

. . . The chill of stanza five is a reflection of the contemplative
mood, as Keats tries to fix permanently what he has seen and felt.
"Cold Pastoral" hits off exactly his new point of view. And in the
famous final lines beginning, "Beauty is truth, truth beauty," he
comes to a satisfying and inevitable conclusion, which could not
have been concretely felt . . . without the powerful physical aid
of empathy.

. . . the *Ode on a Grecian Urn* is a perfect and complete expression of [empathic] processes, which are rooted in strong and vivid
physical sensations, and are capable of growing from this firm and
fertile earth to the highest and most subtle reaches of emotion
and thought.

No. 69 René Wellek and Austin Warren, *Theory of Literature*
(New York: Harcourt, Brace and Company, 1956 [1949]), 99.

If we analyze many famous poems admired for their philosophy,
we frequently discover mere commonplaces concerning man's
mortality or the uncertainty of fate. The oracular sayings of Vic-
torian poets such as Browning, which have struck many readers
as revelatory, often turn out mere portable versions of primeval
truths. Even if we seem to be able to carry away some general
proposition such as Keats' "Beauty Is Truth, Truth Beauty," we
are left to make what we can of these conversible propositions,
unless we see them as the conclusion of a poem which has to do
with illustrating the permanence of art and the impermanence of
human emotions and natural beauty. The reduction of a work
of art to a doctrinal statement—or, even worse, the isolation of
passages—is disastrous to understanding the uniqueness of a work:
it disintegrates its structure and imposes alien criteria of value.

No. 70 C. M. Bowra, *The Romantic Imagination* (Harvard University Press, 1949), 142, 146-148.

In more cases than I care to admit, I have been obliged to gouge
out large areas of scholarly and critical argument in a given work
because of limitations of space. Bowra's essay is a case in point.

The main subject of the "Ode on a Grecian Urn" is the creative ecstasy which the artist perpetuates in a masterpiece. . . .
The poem, which has been concerned with the Urn, ends with a
lesson which all artists have to learn and to which it gives its
special commendation.

The meaning of this message is beyond dispute. Mr. Garrod rightly paraphrases it, "there is nothing real but the beautiful and nothing beautiful but the real." Keats uses "truth," as others do, to mean "reality." He then adds, through the Urn, that this is the only knowledge that we possess and that we need no other. It is the Urn that speaks, and it speaks for a unique kind of experience, of which it states the central essence. The words which Keats gives to the Urn are derived from his own meditations on the nature of his art. He knew that art was not everything, but so far as it concerned him, he was quite consistent about it. . . .

. . . Truth is another name for ultimate reality, and is discovered not by the reasoning mind but by the imagination. The imagination has a special insight into the true nature of things, and Keats accepts its discoveries because they agree with his senses, resolve disagreeable discords, and overwhelm him by their intensity. . . .

The rationale of poetry is that through the imagination it finds something so compelling in its intensity that it is at once both beautiful and real. [This] theory . . . receives its final form in the last lines of the "Ode on a Grecian Urn."

. . . The Ode is his last word on a special activity and a special experience. Within its limits it has its own view of life, and that is what Keats expresses. The belief that "Beauty is truth, truth beauty" is true for the artist while he is concerned with his art. It is no less true that, while he is at work, this is all that he knows for certain and all that he needs to know for the proper pursuit of his special task. Unless he believes this, he is in danger of ruining his art. The "Ode on a Grecian Urn" tells what great art means to those who create it, while they create it, and, so long as this doctrine is not applied beyond its proper confines, it is not only clear but true.

No. 71   F. W. Bateson, *English Poetry: A Critical Introduction* (London: Longmans, Green and Co., 1950), 217-220.

The interest of Keats's poem is that, though explicitly non-political, it is implicitly political. In spite of the Romantic trappings it is not at bottom a wholly Romantic poem.

The Urn, for one thing, is not a symbol in the sense in which the West Wind and Blake's Tiger and Keats's own Nightingale are symbols. There is no question here of an 'objective correlative.' The Urn really only provides an object lesson. By the use of analogies from the Urn Keats is able to make a number of points about the nature of poetry.

The Urn is introduced as comparable with but superior to poetry:

> Sylvan historian, who canst thus express
> A flowery tale more sweetly than our rhyme.

. . . The Urn, then, can beat poetry at its own game. And what that game is is exemplified in the *motionless movement* of l. 9 of stanza I,

> What mad pursuit? What struggle to escape?

Stanza II elaborates the definition with examples of *soundless sound* ('ditties of no tone'), *stationary growth* ('Nor ever can those trees be bare'), and *timeless time* ('For ever wilt thou love and she be fair'). Stanzas III and IV draw certain pathetic and whimsical corollaries, and stanza V sums up the paradox of poetry. As Coleridge, with whom Keats had walked across Hampstead Heath as recently as the previous April, had taught his contemporaries, poetry 'reveals itself in the balance or reconcilement of opposite or discordant qualities. . . .'

The much-debated 'Beauty is truth, truth beauty' must be interpreted in this context. The Urn is a 'Cold Pastoral'; that is to say, like pastoral poetry (the only sense the noun *pastoral* had in the nineteenth century), it is allegorical. Behind the particular unions of opposites depicted on the Urn (motion and immobility, growth and permanence, time and timelessness, etc.) a general synthetic principle is implied. This is the necessity for uniting Romanticism ('beauty') and realism ('truth'), the subconscious with the conscious mind, the feeling with the concept, poetry and philosophy. It is Keats's protest against the Romantic 'split man.' And the point of particular interest is Keats's *social* motive in propounding this generalization. The Urn is 'a friend to man.' The lesson that it teaches will be consolatory to the next generation as well as to Keats's. Indeed, compared to the need for psychological integration other social problems are of secondary importance:

> that is all
> Ye know on earth, and all ye need to know.

Keats oversimplified, of course, but to say, as Allen Tate has done, that stanza V 'is an illicit commentary added by the poet to a "meaning" which was symbolically complete at the end of the preceding stanza' is to miss Keats's point. Stanza IV had been a relapse into Romanticism. The 'green altar,' 'the mysterious priest' and the 'little town' were alluring invitations to reverie. But Keats was too honest to leave it at that. The 'Ode to a Nightingale' had ended with the explicit admission that the 'fancy' is a 'cheat,' and the 'Grecian Urn' concludes with a similar repudiation. But this time it is a positive instead of a negative conclusion. There *is* no escape from the 'woe' that 'shall this generation waste,' but the action of time can be confronted and seen in its proper proportions. To enable its readers to do this is the special function of poetry.

No. 72 Newell F. Ford, *The Prefigurative Imagination of John Keats: A Study of the Beauty-Truth Identification and Its Implications* (Stanford University Press, 1951), 135-140.

This study, like Thorpe's, deals with the beauty-truth identification, but by means of a much different method. The argument throughout is unusually detailed. The nature of both the method and the argument is indicated in these paragraphs from the preface:

Keats's "prefigurative imagination" is not to be understood as the totality of his imagination, but as one strain in his imagination, one current in its flow which, during certain rapturous moments, caused him to identify "beauty" with "truth."

"Take every man hys turn, as for hys tyme." In this book I take my turn in unraveling the meaning of Keats's celebrated identification of "beauty" and "truth." Unraveling is the primary purpose; the secondary purpose is to reinterpret many of the poems in the light of the findings. The justification of another attempt to explain Keats's enigma is, I believe, the use of a method not previously applied to the problem. Clerklike, I began simply by making a concordance of every occurrence of the word "truth" in Keats's writings. Starting with no preconceptions, I hoped to learn whether Keats had left any clues as to his meaning, whether this meaning was traditional and "Platonic" or perhaps private and personal. . . .

No. 73 William Empson, *The Structure of Complex Words* (London: Chatto and Windus, 1951), 368-374.

In substantially the same form, this appeared in the *Sewanee Review* in 1947 as a review of Brooks' *Well-Wrought Urn*, q.v.

[Mr. Cleanth Brooks] treats [the *Grecian Urn*] (in *The Well-Wrought Urn*) as an entirely coherent philosophical position expressed by irony and paradox. . . . But it seems to me to make rather bad philosophy, and rather a dull poem, which the thing need not be. Mr. Brooks dislikes "biography" as a means of explaining verse, since a poem ought to be complete in itself, and he is not very patient with personal expressions of feeling from a writer who is engaged in building one of these complicated structures. It is hard to feel anything very directly about the poem, now that it has been made so much of an "example," but I think it needs to be viewed as a strong if not tragic expression of feeling, and when so viewed is still good.

Mr. Brooks feels that the whole third stanza of the Ode is a falling-off. . . . If we are to try to defend it, says Mr. Brooks, "we shall come nearest success by emphasizing the paradoxical implications of the repeated items. . . . Though the poet has developed and extended his metaphors furthest in this third stanza, the ironic counterpoise is developed furthest too." It seems to me more like dropping an irony; this stanza is concerned to tell us directly about the feelings of Keats. He is extremely *un*-happy, we find, especially about his love affair, but also from the tedium of the pursuit of beauty or pleasure and from the expectation of death. I do not get this from "biography" but from taking the opposites of the three things the stanza calls "happy." Also there is a very dramatic effect, ignored by Mr. Brooks, from the juxtaposition of this stanza with the next:

> . . . *A burning forehead, and a parching tongue.*
> *Who are these coming to the sacrifice?* . . .

It is a cry of awe from the parching tongue, as the poet sees new victims approach, and the stanza goes on to say that none of them will ever go home again, so that their town will be mysteriously desolate. Mr. Brooks has more than a page trying to rationalize this idea, and save it from being thought "an indulgence . . . which is gratuitous and finally silly." . . . But the poet has just told us he is desolate too (if the critic will condescend to notice anything so sentimental); there is a comparison. The idea that the pursuit of beauty eats up the pursuer, who therefore sacrifices himself to it, is really not a remote one for a romantic poet; though I have to admit that I did not realize how directly it was brought in till I tried to think what was wrong with the account of Mr. Brooks. These people's homes will be left desolate because they have gone to make a piece of art-work, and so will Keats' home because he is spending his life on his art. Beauty is both a cause of and an escape from suffering, and in either way suffering is deeply involved in its production. Here is the crisis of the poem; in the sudden exertion of muscle by which Keats skids round the corner from self-pity to an imaginative view of the world. None of these people can get anything out of the world except beauty, and at once we turn back to the pot with a painful ecstasy in the final stanza; there is nothing else left. This is the force behind the cry "Beauty is Truth" (obviously, I think), however the terms of it are to be interpreted.

The chief puzzle about it is that one feels the poem has raised no question about truth before; it is "gratuitous" again; the reconciliation may be all right in itself, but has got hold of the wrong couple. . . . But we cannot suppose that the aphorism is merely dramatic, in the sense of being a suitable remark for a silent pot (suitable only because of its complacence, perhaps). If we were sure that Keats did not agree with the pot the climax would become trivial. . . . It seemed to him, therefore, that the aphorism was *somehow* relevant to the parching tongue, the desolate streets, and the other woes of the generations not yet wasted. He, like his readers, I think, was puzzled by the remarks of the pot, and yet felt that they were very *nearly* intelligible and relevant. . . . It teases us *out of thought;* it stops us thinking; the idea is more suited to a mystical ecstasy than a metaphysical puzzle. And we have reached this condition through a "sacrifice"; for that matter, the usual function of an Urn is to hold the ashes of the dead. What it tells us is a revelation, and revelations are expected to be puzzling. In short, if we recognize the stress of feeling in the rest of the poem, I do not think a reasonable man should withhold his sympathy from the end of it. . . .

However, to say that all this was present for Keats, as a feeling that the pot had summed up a far-reaching mystery, does not say that the lines are good ones, and that the reader ought to feel it too. It often happens that a poet has built his machine, putting all the parts into it and so on very genuinely, and the machine does not go. I think that "Oh Attic shape! Fair attitude! with brede" is a very bad line; the half pun suggesting a false Greek derivation and jammed against an arty bit of Old English seems to me affected and ugly; it is the sort of thing that the snobbish critics of his own time called him a Cockney for. One might feel, as Robert Bridges [Quiller-Couch?] clearly did, that the last lines with their brash attempt to end with a smart bit of philosophy have not got enough knowledge behind them, and are flashy in the same way. I do not feel this myself, only that the effort of seeing the thing as Keats did is too great to be undertaken with pleasure. There is perhaps a puzzle about how far we ought to make this kind of effort, and at what point the size of the effort required simply proves the poem to be bad. But in any case, I do not think the lines need be regarded either as purely Emotive or as a fully detached bit of philosophising.

No. 74 Cleanth Brooks, "Hits and Misses," *Kenyon Review,* XIV (1952), 677.

> Just as Empson had examined unfavorably Brooks' reading of the Ode in his review of *The Well-Wrought Urn* (see No. 73), so Brooks, calling *The Structure of Complex Words* "the most mixed-up book that Empson has written to date," chose to examine unfavorably Empson's interpretation of the poem.

No. 75 Robert M. Adams, *"Trompe-l'oeil* in Shakespeare and Keats," *Sewanee Review,* LXI (1953), 238, 245-247, 251-253.

> Devotees of surrealism will recognize at once the quality of *trompe-l'oeil.* It is a device by which an artist mingles and contrasts different levels of representation. Within the frame of a still-life there may occur, for example, fastened to the surface of the canvas, a literal jack-knife or a prosaic pencil. A figure painted within a frame may be depicted as reaching across the frame to claim existence in a third dimension. . . . Or a series of receding frames may be depicted, as for instance in a picture of a man looking at a painting of a room with a window opening on a landscape—and if, let us say, the sun shining through this painting of a painted window illuminates the face of the painted looker-on, the whole image may be called *trompe-l'oeil.* . . . The device is essentially that of the overstepped or obliterated frame; its effect is to surprise by the incongruity or to impress by the depth of representational levels; and though less frequent in literature than in the plastic arts; it does have an existence on the printed page. . . .
>
> . . . the Odes, which keep meat-and-potatoes reality at a fair esthetic remove, are more successful in handling the device. Their typical structure is that of a vision in a dream, of a discovery made by the mind upon itself. . . .
>
> The "Ode on a Grecian Urn" . . . begins by apostrophizing and interrogating the urn as a shape seen at a distance. Stanza 2 moves our viewpoint subtly enough to within the urn. . . . The next two stanzas . . . are occupied with the elaboration of this contrast, the poem reaching something like a climax with Keats's favorite empathy-word, "warm." . . . But this is no climax comparable to stanza 7 of the "Nightingale" ode; we have not moved far from the surface of things (one frame only has been recessed), and the poetry is relatively thoughtful and undisturbed. The fourth stanza slopes to a conclusion through a quietly declining series of adjectives; the little town, first peaceful, then falls silent and is at last desolate.

Returning to its original attitude of apostrophe from outside, the poem addresses in the . . . final stanza a reproach to the Urn. A silent form, it "teases" us out of thought as does eternity; and while eternity suggests a truthfulness more than human, "teasing" implies a downright deception. The omens are thus balanced; art is eternal but it is not true; it is a higher form of truth but we must be teased into it and cannot remain long under its influence. In stanza 3 the poet *was* thus teased out of thought; but in stanza 5 he clearly is not. . . . [T]he fact that the poet is no longer teased out of thought enables or forces him to see the Urn as a "Cold Pastoral." This muscular image clearly shows the poet within the realm of thought and time and aware of wastage and woe as the urn in its cold, formal eternity cannot be. That the poet should from this point of view foresee the urn's unchanged survival, its eternal murmuring of an unchanging message to changing man, is nothing surprising. . . . The message itself strikes us more oddly, though only a little more so. The urn, which is unalterably of the esthetic sphere, should not and could not talk to us in the commonsense language of men. What it says, then, is spoken from its special point of view; and within that sphere all that is beautiful is true, all that is true is beautiful, and only what is true and beautiful is real. So far we have not burst the bounds of orthodox neo-Platonism. But the last line and a half of the poem . . . —these lines pose a sizable problem. . . . [T]o whom are they addressed? . . . But perhaps the last words of the poem are not spoken *by* but *to* the Urn and the figures on it. . . . The force of the passage is then vindictive; "It's enough for you to say, 'Truth and beauty are the same'—that's your function in the world. But we who are men know this and something else too." Whether or not the passage will bear this sense, the poem's closing remark is clearly intended in the esthetic sphere; it teases us into and out of thought, and in the very act of declaring our alienation from the sphere of the Urn, translates us into it. . . .

No. 76   Alvin Whitley, "The Message of the Grecian Urn," *Keats-Shelley Memorial Bulletin* (London, 1953), V, 1-3.

The message of the Grecian Urn has, unhappily, more often teased critics out of thought than into it. This very brief study . . . seeks . . . by a careful study of the original texts to discover just how the famous apothegm of the urn fits into the poem. In doing so, we may discredit one or two older interpretations and show, at least, what the last lines of the ode cannot mean. . . .

It is from the last stanza and particularly the last two lines that all our critical difficulties spring. . . . One troublesome question has been asked often enough but rarely answered with care: At the very end of the ode, who is saying what to whom? The first published version of the poem, in the *Annals of the Fine Arts,* early in 1820, read:

> Beauty is truth, truth beauty.—That is all
> Ye know on earth, and all ye need to know.

The second appearance of the lines in print, in the *Lamia* volume of 1820, bore slightly different punctuation:

> "Beauty is truth, truth beauty,"—that is all
> Ye know on earth, and all ye need to know.

These readings give rise to three possible interpretations: either both lines are spoken by the urn, but the extra-sententiousness of the first five words merits special pointing; or the first five words are spoken by the urn, the rest by the poet to the reader; or the first five words are spoken by the urn, the rest by the poet to the figures he has just described.

This last contention should die of natural incongruity. It is artistically as well as philosophically unthinkable that Keats would suddenly intrude himself in this way to tell the figures on the urn that they had grasped the one simple regimen of life and need know nothing else, that they were, indeed, probably better off in their pristine ignorance. Keats, to whom the world meant intensely, had no place in his philosophy for noble savages, even Greek ones.

The answer to the riddle of the proper reading, however, lies not in critical speculation but in textual analysis. The two original printings can claim no great authority. The *Annals* text was based on a copy 'begged' of Keats by Haydon, who was not noted for his trustworthiness. As for the *Lamia* version, it is well known that Keats was too ill to oversee the publication of his 1820 volume which was, partially at least, edited by John Taylor.

One must fall back on the manuscripts. Unfortunately no holograph is known to survive, but there are four transcripts, all unquestionably not far removed from the original, and all of them agree.

The transcript by George Keats (in the British Museum) reads:

> Beauty is truth,—Truth Beauty,—that is all
> Ye know on earth, and all ye need to know.

Charles Wentworth Dilke (in his copy of *Endymion,* in the Keats Memorial House, Hampstead):

> Beauty is truth,—truth beauty,—that is all
> Ye know on earth, and all ye need to know.

Charles Armitage Brown (Harvard Keats Collection):

> Beauty is Truth,—Truth Beauty,—that is all
> Ye know on earth, and all ye need to know.

Richard Woodhouse (Harvard):

> Beauty is Truth,—Truth beauty,—That is all
> Ye know on earth, and all ye need to know.

All four transcripts, then, not only lack the full stop and inverted commas of the *Annals* and *Lamia* texts respectively, but they have an additional dash between the two phrases 'Beauty is truth' and 'truth beauty,' thus breaking up the concluding lines of the poem into three rather than two parts. A threefold division must negate completely the possibility of a dual statement which depends on some mechanical indication . . . of the complete integrity of the initial five-word phrase. The transcripts obviously infer a single statement uttered by the urn without any interference on the part of the poet. . . . What the message of the urn may mean is, of course, another matter.

No. 77 Earl Wasserman, *The Finer Tone: Keats' Major Poems* (Baltimore: Johns Hopkins Press, 1953), 58-62.

Neither abridgement nor summary can do justice to this remarkable study. It is meditative, in the best sense, and it undertakes to do what would have been unthinkable before the rise of modern literary criticism and scholarship: to provide a full, a total, reading of a major work of art. The essay on the Grecian Urn is fifty pages long, and I give here only the concluding section. In his "Foreword," Mr. Wasserman explains the method upon which his analysis rests:

It is with no sense of embarrassment, then, that I have used some of Keats' poems to explain others, have combed his letters and other prose for clues to intentions out of which he formed poems, and have even sought aid from a probable "source" poem. I have read the poems as verbal communications, and therefore have searched for relevant information wherever I could find it. I have done so, not only in order to understand the individual words, but especially to discover the presuppositions within which each poem has its being and from which it derives its complex oneness. . . .

If the explications that follow have any validity, it appears to me that Keats emerges from them as one of the great masters of what I choose to call autonomous poetry, poetry whose energy lies within the work itself and is generated by the organic interactions of its component members. This is not the only kind of poetry, for we might distinguish it from, let us say, much of Wordsworth's, whose energy often depends to a greater degree upon the reader's psychological relations to it. . . . Consequently, these two forms of poetry require two different modes of explication. The first must be examined in terms of a living organism, the second in terms of the psychology of an organic experience. . . . I use this explicatory manner here because I believe it corresponds to the peculiar mode of poetic existence possessed by *Keats'* poems; and I believe it corresponds to that mode because I believe that mode is consonant with Keats' metaphysics—not Wordsworth's or mine or anyone else's.

To return now to the concluding lines of the ode. Although the urn is able to reveal to man a oneness of beauty and truth, it is not able to inform him that this is the sum total of his knowledge on earth and that it is sufficient for his earthly existence ("all ye need to know"); for obviously he knows other things on earth, such as the fact that in the world beauty is not truth, and this should be even more valuable within the world than the knowledge that the two are one at heaven's bourne. But more important, the symbolic action of the drama at no point justifies the urn's limiting its message; nowhere has the urn acted out the fact that man knows no more on earth than this identity of beauty and truth, and that this knowledge is sufficient.

Now, it is significant that this is an ode *on* a Grecian urn. Had Keats meant *to,* he would have said so, as he did in the "Ode to a Nightingale." There the meaning of the poem arises out of the dramatic relations of the poet and the symbol; but *on* implies a commentary, and it is Keats who must make the commentary on the drama that he has been observing and experiencing within the urn. It is the poet, therefore, who speaks the words, "that is all / Ye know on earth, and all ye need to know," and he is addressing himself to man, the reader. Hence the shift of reference from "thou" (urn) to "ye" (man). I do not feel the objection frequently raised that if the last line and a half belong to the poet and are addressed to the reader, they are not dramatically prepared for. The poet has gradually been obtruding himself upon the reader's consciousness in the last two stanzas by withdrawing from his empathic experience and taking on identity. He has become distinctly present in the last stanza as a speaker addressing the urn, and proportionately the urn has shrunk from the center of dramatic interest; it is now but a short step for him to turn his address from urn to reader. Moreover, the reader has also been subtly introduced into the stanza, for the poet vividly marks his complete severance from the urn's essence by pluralizing himself ("tease us," "other woe / Than ours") and thus putting himself into a category wholly distinct from the urn; and by this act Keats has now involved the reader as a third member of the drama. Finally, when the reader has been filtered out of the plural "us" and "ours" by the reference to "man" (48), the poet may now address to him his final observations on the drama.

But the poet is no more justified than the urn would be in concluding that the sum of necessary earthly wisdom is the identity of beauty and truth. Certainly when he returned to the dimensional world in stanza four he found the two to be antithetical, not identical. Something of the difficulty Keats encountered in trying to orient his meaning is to be seen in the three versions of the final lines that have manuscript or textual authority. Keats' manuscript and the transcripts made by his friends read,

> *Beauty is truth, truth beauty,—that is all. . . .*

In the *Annals of the Fine Arts* for 1820, where the poem was first published, the line appears as

> *Beauty is Truth, Truth Beauty.—That is all. . . .*

And the 1820 volume of Keats' poems reads,

> *"Beauty is truth, truth beauty,"—that is all. . . .*

No one of these solves the problem, although each hints at the difficulty. Clearly each one strives to separate the aphorism from the following assertion by the poet; and at the same time each attempts to preserve a relation between the pronoun "that" and *something* that has gone before. Then, since we have seen that the antecedent of "that" cannot reasonably be the aphorism—since neither urn nor poet can be saying that all man knows and needs to know on earth is that beauty is truth—its antecedent must be the entire preceding sentence.

All that man knows on earth, and all he needs to know is that

> *When old age shall this generation waste,*
> *Thou [the urn] shalt remain, in midst of other woe*
> *Than ours, a friend to man, to whom thou say'st,*
> *Beauty is truth, truth beauty.*

Only this meaning can be consistent with the dramatic action of the poem, for it not only does not deny that in the world beauty is not truth, but also assimilates that fact into a greater verity. The sum of earthly wisdom is that in this world of pain and decay, where love cannot be forever warm and where even the highest pleasures necessarily leave a burning forehead and a parching tongue, art remains, immutable in its essence because that essence is captured in a "Cold Pastoral," a form which has not been created for the destiny of progressing to a heaven-altar, as warm and passionate man is. This art is forever available as "a friend to man," a power willing to admit man to its "sphery sessions." . . .

The great end of poetry, Keats wrote, is "that it should be a friend / To sooth the cares, and lift the thoughts of man," for art (unlike man, who cannot return to tell us of his postmortal existence) allows a glimpse into that region which shows the full meaning of those experiences which now produce only mortal suffering, divulges the end for which they are destined, and so eases the burden of the mystery. And art eases this burden by holding out to man the promise that somewhere—at heaven's bourne, where the woes of this world will be resolved—songs are forever new, love is forever young, human passion is "human passion far above," beauty is truth; that, although beauty is not truth in this world, what the imagination seizes as beauty must be truth—whether it existed before or not.

The knowledge that in art this insight is forever available is the height of earthly wisdom; and it is all man needs to know, for it endows his earthly existence with a meaning and a purpose. . . .

No. 78 Leo Spitzer, "The 'Ode on a Grecian Urn,' or Content vs. Metagrammar," *Comparative Literature* (1955), 203-225.

Spitzer examines the theoretical bases of Wasserman's reading of the ode, finds them inadequate, and offers his own reading of the poem.

No. 79 E. H. Gombrich, "Visual Metaphors of Value in Art," *Symbols and Values: An Initial Study,* Thirteenth Symposium of the Conference on Science, Philosophy and Religion (New York, 1954), 271-272, 274, 278.

There is no more famous and no more moving record of what we have called the "confluence of values" than Keats's "Ode on a Grecian Urn." It was this (real or imagined) work of art, of course, that inspired the much quoted and much abused utterance, "Beauty is truth, truth beauty." Are we to see more in this poem than a mere exclamation of ecstatic enjoyment? If we read the poem with our present preoccupations in mind, we may be struck by its imagery of gratification withheld, of passion unfulfilled. The very first line introduces this motif:

Thou still unravish'd bride of quietness

and the poem soon rises to that paean of renunciation [in stanzas two and three].

Is it because it is a *"cold"* pastoral, stilled and remote that the urn acquires the dignity of a universal symbol? One may be tempted to think so. For beyond the general neo-platonic faith in the truth of the artist's vision . . . the idea that the realm of beauty can be entered by man only at the price of renunciation plays an important part in eighteenth century esthetics. . . .

But whatever the exact roots and implications of Keats's exclamations there remains the fact that great art has given to many the feeling that they are in the presence of "truth." . . . What we want to know is how we should interpret this intuition that the great work of art is "sincere." . . .

And so we are led to the conclusion that once more it is the submission of the part to the whole, the element of control, of bridled emotion rather than of disconnected symptoms, that is responsible for this intuition of "honesty," which may make art analagous to a moral experience. . . .

Against these positive factors, however, we must set the negative conclusions that might be drawn from some of our observations. The Beauty of the "Grecian Urn" becomes Truth because of what may be called its "plenitude of values" held in miraculous equilibrium—passion and denial, "hot pursuit" in the "cold pastoral." The danger that constantly threatens art from the emergence of new values is precisely the danger to this equilibrium. . . . This process implies, as I have tried to show, that a work of art comes to stand in a context where it is as valued as much for what it rejects and negates as for what it is. . . .

No. 80 Hoxie N. Fairchild, "Comment [on Gombrich's paper],"
Symbols and Values, 280. See above, No. 39.

Keats's "Ode on a Grecian Urn" is more or less climactic in the development of Professor Gombrich's thought, but I cannot help feeling that he has misinterpreted it. The sensuous Keats . . . had no real taste for "passion unfulfilled"; but the unsatisfactoriness of his life finally made him wish to escape from the everyday world . . . into the world of plastic art, where Beauty *can* keep her lustrous eyes precisely because the bold lover will never get his kiss. Here art is not the flower of life, but a heartsick substitute for it. Keats was the most unPlatonic of men. When he says, "Beauty is Truth, Truth Beauty," he means: "All that is true for me, my only reliance in life, is the fact that beautiful objects are beautiful."

But the poem is even sadder than that. "Heard melodies are sweet, but those unheard/Are sweeter." . . . If art is better than life, refraining from art, which after all cannot completely be detached from life, is better than art. Not to make music is better than to make it. Not to make urns is better than to make them. Not to write poems about them is better than to write at all. Inevitably he is drawn toward the final and perfect abstention from gratification:

> Verse, Fame and Beauty are intense indeed,
> But Death intenser—Death is Life's high meed.
> *(Why Did I Laugh Tonight?)*

This is carrying renunciation rather too far for any esthetic, moral, or religious values.

No. 81   Lester Marvin Wolfson, "A Rereading of Keats's Odes: The Intrinsic Approach in Literary Criticism" (unpublished dissertation, University of Michigan, 1954).

By far the most detailed study of all the odes yet written, this thesis provides, in many ways, a summation of most of the major modern critical hypotheses; it makes use of a wide range of methods and concepts which, in our time, have become established, even commonplace. I give below a number of statements from the introduction in which the author explains his purpose:

The purpose of this paper is to examine the odes as literary structures, or systems of signs ideally organized toward a specific aesthetic purpose. I propose to intermingle the scientific and artistic methods of criticism, the analytic and synthetic. . . . The crucial matter for a full comprehension of what poetry is appears to be a right understanding of metaphor. . . . Of almost equal importance . . . is a correct understanding of the total phonetic pattern of poetry. . . . The right experiencing of a poem is qualitatively different from the experiencing of anything not a poem, and is approximated only by reactions to the other arts. . . . But there is only one scale for judging ultimate worth, and that is whether a thing does or does not contribute to the totality of our normative adjustment to life [for a poem is cognitive as well as emotive]. . . . It is within this Judaeo-Christian framework that my own judgments of the odes are made . . . [for] intrinsic criticism may legitimately evaluate the worth of a poem's discursive meaning. . . . [Intrinsic criticism] is the attempt of the critic to investigate the poem itself as a linguistic construct which has the objective power to control the responses which are appropriate to it. . . .

No. 82   Robert Gittings, *John Keats: The Living Year* (London: Heinemann, 1954).

An exciting and controversial biography of Keats, which attempts to reconstruct in detail what Keats did, read and thought during the twelve month period in which he wrote almost all of his greatest poems.

No. 83 Philip Wheelwright, *The Burning Fountain: A Study in the Language of Symbolism* (University of Indiana Press, 1954), 300-302.

The greater uses of depth language, as exemplified in religion, in poetry, and in myth, represent approximately the scope and focus of this book; whose central thesis . . . is that religious, poetic, and mythic utterances at their best really mean something, make a kind of objective reference, although neither the objectivity nor the method of referring is of the same kind as in the language of science. (p. 4.)

No. 84 K. M. Hamilton, "Time and the Grecian Urn," *The Dalhousie Review,* XXXIV (Autumn 1954), 246-254.

No. 85 Charles I. Patterson, "Passion and Permanence in Keats's *Ode on a Grecian Urn,*" *English Literary History,* XXI (Sept. 1954), 208-220.

No. 86 Robert C. Fox, "Keats' ODE ON A GRECIAN URN, I-IV," *Explicator* (June 1956), 58.

No. 87 Alwyn Berland, "Keats's Dark Passages and the Grecian Urn," *Kansas Magazine* (1956), 78-82.

No. 88 Jacob D. Wigod, "Keats's Ideal in the Ode on a Grecian Urn," *PMLA,* LXXII (March 1957), 113-121.

This article is a useful summary and critique of recent writing on the ode; below is the author's opening paragraph:

Rooted in awareness of pain and flux, Keats's odes of 1819 reveal the poet's desire to escape the painful actual and seek repose in beauty, in the ideal. More than any other of the odes, the implicit subject of the Ode on a Grecian Urn is the ideal itself. While the permanance of art is the poet's bulwark against flux, it is not the ultimate perfection that he seeks. Too many inner tensions, as the poem develops, shape the ideal into something much more complex, unattainable in either life or art since it encompasses *both* life and art. Keats's attempt to define this ideal accounts for the difficulty of the concluding lines. The purpose of this paper is to try to illuminate Keats's mode of thought and feeling as he wrote the poem and thereby, perhaps, to approach more closely his meaning.

Author Index to Chapter Three